THE ULTIMATE
UNOFFICIAL CHELSEA QUIZ BOOK
1905 QUIZ QUESTIONS

CHELSEA CHADDER

The Ultimate Unofficial Chelsea Quiz Book
1905 Quiz Questions
Copyright: Chelsea Chadder 2020
ISBN: 979-8562592927

Twitter: @ChelseaChadder
Cover design: Will Hopkins
www.gate17.co.uk

DEDICATION

To my three wonderful kids. You make me so proud.

You are the future of Chelsea Football Club and will be a part of their history.

All my love,

Daddy xXx

PREFACE

Are you a Chelsea fan or know someone who is? Test your knowledge of the club with this ultimate unofficial Chelsea quiz book. It contains 1,905 questions about the Blues covering over one hundred years of history.

- What is the name of Chelsea's stadium?
- Who did Chelsea play in their first ever competitive game?
- In what year did Luiz Felipe Scolari become the Blues manager?
- Which Blues striker had footballing brothers called Brian and Edwin?

With over 90 different categories this book will test even the most hardcore Chelsea fan. It will help you to learn things about the club that you've never known or just forgotten over time. The quiz categories range from London rivals, managers, players such as Frank Lampard and Didier Drogba to general Chelsea knowledge.

Written by the author of other Chelsea titles including 'Chelsea: 100 Memorable Matches' and 'Chelsea: If Twitter Was Around When...', @ChelseaChadder has written this quiz book using his extensive knowledge about the club he loves – Chelsea Football Club.

Starter Questions

You think you know Chelsea? Are you a true Blue? Start by trying to answer these five simple questions about the football club. The answers to each quiz are on the next page.

1. In what year were Chelsea formed?
2. What is the name of Chelsea's stadium?
3. What is the club's nickname?
4. Who did Chelsea play in their first ever competitive game?
5. Who scored the winning penalty in the 2012 Champions League final shootout?

General Knowledge 1

This round tests your Chelsea general knowledge. These are questions that most Blues fans should know but how many will you get correct?

1. Who became Chelsea's manager in 2019?
2. Who bought the club in 2003?
3. Who became Chelsea's all-time leading appearance maker in 1980 with 795 games?
4. What are the names of the two Chelsea mascots?
5. In which year did John Terry make his debut for the Blues?
6. Which country did Petr Cech represent?
7. In what year did Chelsea first win the Premier League?
8. Which company started making the Blues kit in 2017?
9. Who was the club's first £1m+ signing?
10. Who became Chelsea's all-time leading goalscorer in 2014 with 211 goals?
11. What is Chelsea's highest official attendance at Stamford Bridge?
12. What is the club's highest aggregate win in European football?
13. What was the name of the pub where Chelsea were formed?
14. What was the name of the family that originally owned Chelsea FC?
15. Who is known as The King of Stamford Bridge?
16. The North Stand at Stamford Bridge is named after which former club director?
17. Who sang the lead vocals on the club's 1997 FA Cup final song?
18. Who bought the Blues for £1 back in 1982?
19. Which team did Chelsea beat in the 2012 Champions League final?
20. What is the nationality of Roman Abramovich?

1 1905 2 Stamford Bridge 3 The Blues 4 Stockport County 5 Didier Drogba

True or False 1

Read the following questions. Just simply answer True or False for each question.

1. Chelsea captain John Harris was the brother of future skipper Ron Harris.

2. The Blues have played every single one of their home games at Stamford Bridge.

3. Dan Petrescu's youngest daughter is called Chelsea.

4. Ray Wilkins is the youngest person to captain Chelsea.

5. Stamford Bridge is built next to a cemetery.

6. Jose Mourinho had a dog called Gullit.

7. Chelsea were the first English team to compete in the European Cup.

8. Chelsea were the first side to wear shirt numbers.

9. Vivian Woodward was a Chelsea goalkeeper.

10. Fernando Torres was the first person to score for and against Chelsea in the Premier League during the same season.

11. Swiss international defender, Willi Steffen, had been a fighter pilot during the Second World War.

12. Willi Steffen's English teacher was the wife of Chelsea manager Billy Birrell.

13. Chelsea have always had a lion on their club badge.

14. Chelsea once wore Coventry City shirts in a Premier League game.

15. Chelsea's first ever manager was English.

16. Chelsea were the first football team to play at the new Yankee Stadium.

17. The Blues were the first English team to be involved in a game using

goal line technology.

18. Tommy Docherty was Chelsea manager when the Blues won the league in 1955.

19. Ryan Bertrand made his European debut in the 2012 Champions League final.

20. Chelsea used to have the nickname 'The Pensioners'.

Answers from quiz General Knowledge 1

1 Frank Lampard 2 Roman Abramovich 3 Ron Harris 4 Stamford and Bridget 5 1998 6 Czech Republic 7 2005 8 Nike 9 Dennis Wise 10 Frank Lampard 11 82,905 12 21-0 13 The Rising Sun 14 Mears 15 Peter Osgood 16 Matthew Harding 17 Suggs 18 Ken Bates 19 Bayern Munich 20 Russian

2010s Chelsea

This set of questions is all about Chelsea in the 2010s decade. How well do you know you club?

1. Who did Chelsea beat in the 2015 League Cup final?

2. In which country did the Blues win the 2012 Champions League final?

3. In what year did Kevin De Bruyne sign for Chelsea?

4. Which former Blues manager was in charge of Portsmouth in the 2010 FA Cup final?

5. How many people played for Chelsea in both the 2012 and 2019 Europa League finals?

6. Who did the Blues sign from Leicester City in 2017?

7. In what year did Diego Costa leave Chelsea?

8. Andre Villas-Boas was sacked after losing to which team?

9. In which country did Chelsea win the 2018/19 Europa League final?

10. Who scored a hattrick for the Blues against BATE Borisov in 2018?

11. In which year was John Terry stripped of the England captaincy?

12. Who was the Blues manager when they won the Premier League in 2015?

13. Which Stoke City player scored two own goals in one game against Chelsea in January 2013?

14. How many games did Rob Green play for the Blues?

15. What country did Christian Pulisic represent?

16. Which former Chelsea player appeared for Arsenal in the 2019 Europa League final?

17. In what year did Ashley Cole win his 100th cap for England?

18. The Blues signed Mohammed Salah from which club?

19. What squad number did Gary Cahill wear with Chelsea?

20. Who were the Blues opponents when they first played a game using goal line technology in 2012?

1 False 2 True 3 True 4 False 5 True 6 True 7 False 8 True 9 False 10 False 11 True 12 True 13 False 14 True 15 False 16 True 17 True 18 False 19 True 20 True

Africans

Football is a world game and part of Chelsea's history includes Africa. How many of these themed related questions can you get right?

1. Who was the first African to play for Chelsea?
2. Who was the first African to score for the Blues?
3. Celestine Babayaro played for which country?
4. George Weah scored on his Chelsea debut. Who were the opponents?
5. Which Chelsea player came from Burkino Faso?
6. Which MLS team did Didier Drogba play for?
7. What was the name of the American team that Didier Drogba became a minority owner of?
8. Which African crossed the ball in for John Arne Riise to score an own goal for Chelsea against Liverpool?
9. In which African country was Mark Stein born?
10. Which African played for Ghana in the 2006 World Cup?
11. After leaving Chelsea, which other English side did Geremi join?
12. Who is the Blues only Senegalese international?
13. Papy Djilobodji only played once for Chelsea. Who were the opponents?
14. Which Chelsea player represented Egypt?
15. Victor Moses signed for the Blues from which club side?
16. Samuel Eto'o joined the Blues from which club side?
17. Which African scored for the Blues after Steven Gerrard slipped during a

Chelsea vs Liverpool match?

18. Ola Aina represented England at youth level but which country did he play for at senior level?

19. How many times was Didier Drogba sent off for Chelsea?

20. Baba Rahman played for which country?

Answers from quiz 2010s Chelsea

1 Tottenham 2 Germany 3 2012 4 Avram Grant 5 Two 6 Danny Drinkwater 7 2017 8 West Brom 9 Azerbaijan 10 Ruben Loftus-Cheek 11 2012 12 Jose Mourinho 13 Jon Walters 14 Zero 15 USA 16 Petr Cech 17 2013 18 FC Basel 19 24 20 Monterrey

Who Are Ya? 1

Read the clues to work out which person from the Blues history it is talking about.

1. Born in 1966 and was the first person ever to play in FA Cup finals in three different decades.

2. Signed from Parma in 2003 and sacked for taking cocaine.

3. A legendary goalkeeper weighing over 20 stone.

4. Sold twice from the Blues and won the Premier League with Blackburn in 1995.

5. Signed for Chelsea twice but originally bought from Marseille in 2004.

6. Won the World Cup in 1998 and moved to Al Gharafa in 2004.

7. The first person to score a hattrick in a Wembley cup final since Geoff Hurst in 1966.

8. Sold to Man Utd and the first ever Englishman to be sent off in a World Cup.

9. Won the Premier League with Chelsea after loan spells with Liverpool,

Stoke and West Ham.

10. Signed for the Blues on the same day as Fernando Torres.

11. A German who won the World Cup in 2014 whilst with Chelsea.

12. Signed for Chelsea in 1978 and famous for being able to throw a gold ball the length of a football pitch.

13. Wore every shirt number for the Blues from 1 to 12, except number 11.

14. Scored 110 goals for Chelsea between 2012 and 2019.

15. Sign from PSV and scored in the 2005 League Cup final.

16. Once received a red card with Chelsea in 2007 after celebrating a goal.

17. First black manager to win the FA Cup.

18. Scored Denmark's first ever international goal back in 1908.

19. Captained of Russia at the 1994 World Cup.

20. Won the World Cup in 2002 and the Premier League in 2010.

Answers from quiz Africans

1 Ralph Oelofse 2 Derek Smethurst 3 Nigeria 4 Tottenham 5 Bertrand Traore 6 Montreal Impact 7 Phoenix Rising 8 Salomon Kalou 9 South Africa 10 Michael Essien 11 Newcastle Utd 12 Papy Djilobodji 13 Walsall 14 Mohammed Salah 15 Wigan Athletic 16 Anzhi Makhachkala 17 Demba Ba 18 Nigeria 19 Five 20 Ghana

Arsenal

Arsenal are one of Chelsea's biggest rivals and there have been some classic encounters between the two clubs. Have a go at answering these themed questions.

1. In which year did Chelsea first play Arsenal?

2. What was the score when the Blues beat Arsenal in the 2019 Europa League final?

3. Which former Blues was in goal for Arsenal in that match?

4. How many players were sent off when the two teams met in the 2006/07 League Cup final?

5. Which player was sent off in the 2017 FA Cup final?

6. Which player scored in his last appearance for the Blues in the same game?

7. Who lost 6-0 to Chelsea in his 1,000th game as a manger in 2014?

8. How many goals did Didier Drogba score for the Blues against Arsenal?

9. Chelsea inflicted Arsenal's biggest ever defeat at Highbury. What was the scoreline?

10. Who got a red card for punching Martin Keown in a match at Stamford Bridge in 1995?

11. Who scored for both teams in an FA Cup quarter final in 2003?

12. Who did Chelsea sign from Arsenal at the start of the 2006/07 season?

13. Which Blues defender moved the other way?

14. Who scored four goals for the Blues against Arsenal in 1964?

15. Who played for the Blues in the 1971 UEFA Cup Winners Cup final and for Arsenal in 1980?

16. Which manager knocked Arsenal out of the 2003/04 Champions League?

17. Peter Bonetti played his final game for Chelsea, against Arsenal, in what year?

18. Who scored a thunderous equaliser for the Blues against Arsenal at Stamford Bridge in December 2006?

19. Which player won the FA Cup with Arsenal in 2005 and again with Chelsea in 2018?

20. Who played for both clubs before dying in 2001 aged just 33?

Answers from quiz Who Are Ya?

1 Dennis Wise 2 Adrian Mutu 3 Willie Foulke 4 Graeme Le Saux 5 Didier Drogba 6 Marcel Desailly 7 David Speedie 8 Ray Wilkins 9 Victor Moses 10 David Luiz 11 Andre Schurrle 12 Duncan McKenzie 13 David Webb 14 Eden Hazard 15 Mateja Kezman 16 Arjen Robben 17 Ruud Gullit 18 Nils Middelboe 19 Dmitri Kharine 20 Juliano Belletti

General Knowledge 2

This round tests your Chelsea general knowledge. These are questions that most Blues fans should know but how many will you get correct?

1. Who is the only player to score six goals for Chelsea in one match?

2. Who was Chelsea's first ever goalkeeper?

3. Which trophy did the Blues win in 1965?

4. Who were the opponents in the final?

5. Who is the only goalkeeper to score for Chelsea?

6. What nationality was Nils Middelboe was the club's first overseas player?

7. In which year did the Blues first wear shirt numbers?

8. Who scored Chelsea's first ever goal in the Premier League?

9. In 1945, the Blues played in front of an estimated crowd of 100,000. Who were the opponents?

10. Who was the first Chelsea player to play in a World Cup?

11. Who was Chelsea's manager when they won the league in 1955?

12. In what year did the Blues play in their first competitive European game?

13. Jimmy Greaves left Chelsea in 1961. Which club did he sign for?

14. Who was the first person to play as a substitute for Chelsea?

15. Who scored in the first minute for the Blues in the 1997 FA Cup final?

16. What was memorable about Chelsea's starting line-up against

Southampton on Boxing Day 1999?

17. Chelsea won the 1998 UEFA Super Cup against Real Madrid. Who scored the only goal of the game?

18. Which Chelsea player scored a famous goal in a 1-1 draw against AC Milan in the San Siro?

19. The Blues won the FA Cup in 2000. Who were the opponents?

20. In 2008, who was given the title of Life President of Chelsea?

Answers from quiz Arsenal

1 1907 2 4-1 3 Petr Cech 4 Three 5 Victor Moses 6 Diego Costa 7 Arsene Wenger 8 Thirteen 9 5-0 10 Nigel Spackman 11 John Terry 12 Ashley Cole 13 William Gallas 14 Bobby Tambling 15 John Hollins 16 Claudio Ranieri 17 1979 18 Michael Essien 19 Cesc Fabregas 20 David Rocastle

Family Connection

One of the most common reasons that Chelsea fans support the club is through a family connection. How many of these theme related questions can you get right?

1. What were the names of the Mears brothers who formed Chelsea back in 1905?

2. What is the name of Ron Harris' footballing brother who also played for Chelsea?

3. Which Chelsea manager also had a son of the same name who played for the club?

4. What was the surname of the Blues footballing brothers Graham and Ray?

5. In which stand is the Family stand situated at Stamford Bridge?

6. Who are the only father and son combination to play for Chelsea?

7. John Hollins had a goalkeeping brother. What was his name?

8. John played for England. Which country did Dave represent?

9. Which former Tottenham midfielder is the cousin of Frank Lampard?

10. Who is the adopted father of Shaun Wright-Phillips?

11. Which Chelsea player had brothers called Kylian and Thorgan?

12. Which player's father and grandfather have both won La Liga?

13. Who made his international debut in 1996 after coming on as a substitute for his own father?

14. Which Chelsea played, signed from Rangers in 1998, played international football with his brother Michael?

15. Seth Adonkor is the half-brother of which Chelsea captain?

16. What is the name of Pat Nevin's cousin who captained England?

17. Former Assistant Manager, Paul Clement had a son who played for Chelsea. What was his son's name?

18. What is the name of the TV presenter that married Frank Lampard in 2015?

19. Ashley Cole married a member of which UK girl band?

20. Which Blues striker had footballing brothers called Brian and Edwin?

Answers from quiz General Knowledge 2

1 George Hilsdon 2 Willie 'Fatty' Foulke 3 The League Cup 4 Leicester City 5 Ben Howard Baker 6 Danish 7 1928 8 Mick Harford 9 Dynamo Moscow 10 Roy Bentley 11 Ted Drake 12 1958 13 AC Milan 14 John Boyle 15 Roberto Di Matteo 16 All the players were from overseas 17 Gustavo Poyet 18 Dennis Wise 19 Aston Villa 20 Lord Richard Attenborough

Champions League

The Champions League is the holy grail of European football. Have a go at answering these Champions League questions about Chelsea.

1. In which stadium did Chelsea win the Champions League in 2012?

2. Who did the Blues play in their first ever Champions League game?

3. Which player scored the club's first goal in the competition?

4. Who was sent off in the 2008 Champions League final?

5. Who scored the final goal in a 2-2 draw at the Nou Camp in the 2012 semi-final?

6. What was the name of the referee who denied Chelsea several penalties in a game against Barcelona at Stamford Bridge in 2009?

7. Which club eliminated the Blues at the semi-final stage in 2004?

8. Who did Chelsea beat 6-0 in the 2014/15 season of the competition?

9. Who was the first player to be sent off for the Blues in the Champions League?

10. At what stage were Chelsea knocked out in their first Champions League campaign in the 1999/2000 season?

11. What was the score when the Blues faced AC Milan in the San Siro in 1999?

12. Which manager led the Blues to their first Champions League final?

13. Who scored for Chelsea in the 2008 final?

14. The Blues also beat Qarabag by the same scoreline in 2017. Which country do Qarabag come from?

15. Which Chelsea goalkeeper was on loan at Atletico Madrid when the Spaniards beat the Blues in the 2014 semi-final?

16. Which team knocked Chelsea out of the competition in 2015 and 2016?

17. Which German team did the Blues face in the 2007/08 group stage?

18. The two clubs met in the 2014/16 season. Which former Blues was manager of Schalke for game at the Veltins Arena?

19. Who won the Premier League with Chelsea and faced the club as manager with Maccabi Tel Aviv in 2015?

20. Who was the only Chelsea player to miss in the 2012 final penalty shootout?

1 Joseph and Gus 2 Allan Harris 3 David Calderhead 4 Wilkins 5 East Stand 6

Les and Clive Allen 7 Dave Hollins 8 Wales 9 Jamie Redknapp 10 Ian Wright

11 Eden Hazard 12 Marcos Alonso 13 Eidur Gudjohnsen 14 Brian Laudrup 15

Marcel Desailly 16 Terry Butcher 17 Neil Clement 18 Christine Bleakley 19

Girls Aloud 20 Mark Stein

True or False 2

Read the following questions. Just simply answer True or False for each question.

1. Chelsea won the Champions League in 2012.

2. Stamford Bridge was built in 1905.

3. Stamford Bridge is in the King's Road.

4. Chelsea's mascots are called Stamford & Bridget.

5. Jose Mourinho managed Chelsea in two different spells.

6. Eden Hazard and Micky Hazard are related.

7. Dick Spence is the oldest person to play for the Blues.

8. Petr Cech played over 500 games for Chelsea.

9. Terry Venables was once the Chelsea manager.

10. Jimmy Greaves scored 43 goals for the Blues in the 1960/61 season.

11. Chelsea have never played on Christmas Day.

12. Mario Stanic scored on his Chelsea debut.

13. Jimmy Floyd Hasselbaink joined the Blues from Leeds Utd.

14. Keith Weller scored for Chelsea after just 12 seconds in a game vs Middlesbrough in 1970.

15. In 1905, the Blues played twice on the same day.

16. In 1920, Chelsea signed a qualified doctor who went on to score 10 goals for the Blues.

17. Queen Elizabeth II once watched a Chelsea match at Stamford Bridge.

18. Blue is the Colour' was released in 1970 for the FA Cup final.

19. Stamford Bridge used to host greyhound racing.

20. Peter Bonetti was born in Italy.

Answers from quiz Champions League

1 Allianz Arena 2 Skonto Riga 3 Celestine Babayaro 4 Didier Drogba 5 Fernando Torres 6 Tom Henning Ovrebo 7 Monaco 8 Maribor 9 Chris Sutton 10 Quarter final 11 1-1 12 Avram Grant 13 Frank Lampard 14 Azerbaijan 15 Thibaut Courtois 16 PSG 17 Schalke 04 18 Roberto Di Matteo 19 Slavisa Jokanovic 20 Juan Mata

Squad Numbers

Some players and their shirt numbers are synonymous while others are forgotten. How much do you know about Chelsea players and their squad numbers?

1. What is the name of the first Chelsea player to be given the number 1 squad number?

2. Branislav Ivanovic wore the number 2 shirt. What nationality was he?

3. Who was the first non-Englishman to be given the number 3 shirt?

4. Who was the last player to be given the number 4 shirt before Claude Makelele?

5. Which Chelsea player was given the number 23 shirt for ten seasons?

6. Who is the only Dutchman to be given the number 6 shirt?

7. In 1998, two Chelsea players were both given the number 7 shirt. Brian Laudrup was one but who was the other?

8. Who was given the number 8 shirt after Frank Lampard left Chelsea?

9. Tony Cascarino was first player to be given the number 9 squad number.

Which international country did he play for?

10. Which Italian striker only scored once for Chelsea in the Premier League whilst wearing the number 10 shirt?

11. Didier Drogba wore the number 11 shirt and which other number in his Chelsea career?

12. Mario Stanic wore the number 12 shirt for his Premier League debut and scored a wonder goal. Who were the opponents?

13. Which player was given the number 13 shirt before it was given to Michael Ballack?

14. Andre Schurrle was given the number 14 shirt. In which year did he win the World Cup?

15. Who wore the number 15 shirt for Chelsea in the 2013/14 season?

16. Which Chelsea manager wore the number 16 shirt as a player?

17. When Eden Hazard first joined Chelsea he was given the number 17 shirt. Who had worn it before him?

18. Who wore the number 18 shirt for the Blues in the 1997 FA Cup final?

19. Which Chelsea youth product was the first to wear the number 19 shirt?

20. Which player to the number 20 shirt in the 2003/04 season?

Answers from quiz True or False 2

1 True 2 False 3 In 1982, Ken Bates bought Chelsea for £1. 4 True 5 True 6 False 7 True 8 False 9 False 10 True 11 False 12 False 13 False 14 True 15 True 16 True 17 False 18 False 19 True 20 False

Previous Club 1

Look at the players in this set of questions. From which club did Chelsea sign them from?

1. Kepa Arrizabalaga
2. Ross Barkley
3. Pedro
4. Olivier Giroud
5. Mateo Kovacic
6. Jorginho
7. Cesar Azpilicueta
8. N'Golo Kante
9. Marcos Alonso
10. Kurt Zouma
11. Antonio Rudiger
12. Willian
13. Michy Batshuayi
14. Christian Pulisic
15. Emerson Palmieri
16. Tiemoue Bakayoko
17. Davide Zappacosta
18. Ethan Ampadu
19. Danny Drinkwater
20. Alvaro Morata

Answers from quiz Squad Numbers

1 Dmitri Kharine 2 Serbian 3 Celestine Babayaro 4 Jes Hogh 5 Carlo Cudicini 6 Nathan Ake 7 Bjarne Goldbaek 8 Oscar 9 Republic of Ireland 10 Pierluigi Casiraghi 11 15 12 West Ham 13 William Gallas 14 2014 15 Kevin De Bruyne 16 Roberto Di Matteo 17 Jose Bosingwa 18 Eddie Newton 19 Neil Shipperley 20 Juan Sebastian Veron

2000s Chelsea

This set of questions is all about Chelsea in the 2000s decade. How well do you know you club?

1. Who scored the winning goal in the 2000 FA Cup final?

2. Against which team did Chelsea beat to clinch their first Premier League title back in 2005?

3. In which year did Michael Ballack sign for the Blues?

4. Who did Chelsea beat on penalties in the 2009 Community Shield?

5. In 2002 who became the first person to score 50 Premier League goals for the Blues?

6. Which country did Jose Bosingwa represent?

7. Who scored for the Blues in the 2006 Community Shield?

8. What team did Chelsea beat 6-0 in the Premier League during the 2007/08 season?

9. In which year did Dennis Wise make his final appearance for the Blues?

10. Which country did Mark Bosnich represent?

11. What shirt number did Robert Huth wear with the Blues?

12. Who scored a hattrick for Chelsea against Watford in Ray Wilkins only game in temporary charge as manager?

13. In what year did Luiz Felipe Scolari become the Blues manager?

14. Two Chelsea players were sent off on Boxing Day 2007. Who were the opponents?

15. Who was the Blues boss at the end of the decade?

16. Scott Sinclair scored his only goal for Chelsea against which club?

17. In what year did Alexey Smertin sign for the Blues?

18. In 2004 who became the first Chelsea player to score at a European Championships?

19. Whose penalty did Petr Cech save in the 2008 Champions League final penalty shootout?

20. In what year did Peter Osgood pass away?

Answers from quiz Previous Club 1

1 Atletico Bilbao 2 Everton 3 Barcelona 4 Arsenal 5 Real Madrid 6 Napoli 7 Marseille 8 Leicester 9 Fiorentina 10 Saint Etienne 11 Roma 12 Anzhi Makhachkala 13 Marseille 14 Borussia Dortmund 15 Roma 16 Monaco 17 Torino 18 Exeter City 19 Leicester 20 Real Madrid

Goalkeepers

There have been many great goalkeepers in the Blues history. Have a go at answering these shot stopping related questions.

1. Who was the Chelsea goalkeeper when they won the Champions League in 2012?

2. Petr Cech saved a penalty in the final from which former Chelsea player?

3. Who was the first ever Chelsea goalkeeper?

4. Which goalkeeper scored a penalty for the Blues in 1921?

5. Who played in goal for Chelsea in the 1970 FA Cup final?

6. Which goalkeeper saved two penalties in the same game vs Manchester Utd in 1986?

7. Which goalkeeper ended his career at Chelsea at the age of just 28 due to injuries?

8. Which country did Petar Borota represent at international level?

9. Which goalkeeper refused to be substituted in the 2019 League Cup final?

10. Who kept a clean sheet against Barcelona on his Chelsea debut in 2006?

11. Craig Forrest played for the Blues in 1997 whilst on loan from which club?

12. Who played in goal for Chelsea in the FA Cup final win in 2000?

13. Who went in goal vs Reading after Petr Cech and Carlo Cudicini went off injured?

14. Kevin Hitchcock was sent off against Sheffield Wednesday in 1991. Which player replaced him in goal?

15. Who was the first goalkeeper to be sent off for Chelsea in the Premier League?

16. Which keeper played 157 times for the Blues and later became the club's physio?

17. Which goalkeeper conceded two Eric Cantona penalties in the 1994 FA Cup final?

18. Which goalkeeper conceded twice against Chelsea in the 1998 League Cup final and later played for the Blues?

19. Who was Chelsea's goalkeeper in their first FA Cup final in 1915?

20. Which goalkeeper did the Blues sign from Mansfield Town?

Answers from quiz 2000s Chelsea

1 Roberto Di Matteo 2 Bolton 3 2006 4 Manchester Utd 5 Gianfranco Zola 6 Portugal 7 Andriy Shevchenko 8 Manchester City 9 2001 10 Australia 11 29 12 Nicolas Anelka 13 2008 14 Aston Villa 15 Carlo Ancelotti 16 Hull City 17 2003 18 Frank Lampard 19 Ronaldo 20 2006

Manchester Utd

Manchester Utd are one of Chelsea's biggest rivals and there have been some classic encounters between the two clubs. Have a go at answering these themed questions.

1. Which Chelsea manager became the Manchester Utd boss in 2016?

2. Who played for Man Utd and Chelsea whilst on loan from Monaco between 2014 and 2016?

3. In which year did the Blues first play Man Utd?

4. Which player scored in both 1-0 wins vs Manchester Utd in the 1993/94 season?

5. Who did Chelsea sign from Man Utd in 1992?

6. In which country did the two clubs meet in the 2008 Champions League final?

7. What was the score after 90 minutes?

8. Jose Mourinho's first ever game as Chelsea manager was against Man Utd in 2004. How many players made their Blues debut?

9. Who won the Champions League with Chelsea before moving to Man Utd in 2014?

10. Who was the referee in the 1994 FA Cup final?

11. Which player scored a hattrick for the Blues against Man Utd in 2014?

12. What was the score when Chelsea played Man Utd at Stamford Bridge in October 1999?

13. Which player was sent off in the game?

14. Who scored an own goal in that match?

15. Who scored a hattrick for Chelsea on his debut vs Man Utd in 1954?

16. The Blues signed Mark Hughes from Man Utd in 1995. How much was the transfer fee?

17. Paul Scholes and which Chelsea player were both sent off in an FA Cup quarter final match in 1999?

18. Bobby Charlton lost in his last game for Man Utd against Chelsea in 1973. Who scored the only goal of the game?

19. In the Blues title winning season of 1954/55 Chelsea lost at home to Man Utd. How many goals did the Blues score?

20. Who scored against Man Utd in his final game for Chelsea back April 2000?

Answers from quiz Goalkeepers

1 Petr Cech 2 Arjen Robben 3 Willie Foulke 4 Ben Howard Baker 5 Peter Bonetti 6 Tony Godden 7 Eddie Niedzwiecki 8 Yugoslavia 9 Kepa Arrizabalaga 10 Henrique Hilario 11 Ipswich Town 12 Ed De Goey 13 John Terry 14 Vinnie Jones 15 Frode Grodas 16 Harry Medhurst 17 Dmitri Kharine 18 Mark Schwarzer 19 Jim Molyneux 20 Kevin Hitchcock

Next Club 1

Look at the players in this set of questions. Name the club they joined after leaving Chelsea.

1. Eden Hazard

2. John Terry

3. Gary Cahill

4. Cesc Fabregas

5. Diego Costa

6. Nathaniel Chalobah

7. Branislav Ivanovic

8. Oscar

9. Petr Cech

10. Mohamed Salah

11. Andre Schurrle

12. Fernando Torres

13. Demba Ba

14. Juan Mata

15. Ryan Bertrand

16. Romelu Lukaku

17. Oriol Romeu

18. Daniel Sturridge

19. Raul Meireles

20. Alex

1 Jose Mourinho 2 Radamel Falcao 3 1905 4 Gavin Peacock 5 Mal Donaghy 6 Russia 7 1-1 8 Six 9 Juan Mata 10 David Elleray 11 Samuel Eto'o 12 5-0 13 Nicky Butt 14 Henning Berg 15 Seamus O'Connell 16 £1.5m 17 Roberto Di Matteo 18 Peter Osgood 19 Five 20 Dan Petrescu

South America

Football is a world game and part of Chelsea's history includes South America. How many of these themed related questions can you get right?

1. Who was the first South American to play for Chelsea?

2. Who was the only South American to play for Chelsea in the 2012 Champions League final?

3. Which Brazilian scored in the 2012 FA Cup final?

4. Which player scored a winning goal in the Champions League final in 2006 and joined the Blues a year later?

5. For what country did Gonzalo Higuain represent?

6. Which Colombian played for Chelsea in the 2015 League Cup final?

7. How many goals did Juan Sebastian Veron score for the Blues?

8. In which year did Willian make his Chelsea debut?

9. Which South American scored against the Blues for Bayern Munich in 2005?

10. From which club did Chelsea sign Emerson Thome?

11. How many appearances did Mineiro make for Chelsea?

12. Which Brazilian missed a penalty in a game where the Blues beat Aston Villa 8-0 in 2012?

13. Who was the first South American to play in goal for Chelsea?

14. Which Brazilian won the Chelsea Goal of the Season award in 2013 and

2015?

15. Which South American player scored his only goal for the Blues in April 2016?

16. Who was the only South American to play for Chelsea in the 2005/06 league winning season?

17. Which manager gave Alex his Blues debut?

18. Filipe Luis only scored one goal for Chelsea. Who were the opponents?

19. Which Argentinian was an unused substitute for the Blues in the 2009 FA Cup final?

20. Who beat Chelsea in the 2012 FIFA Club World Cup final?

Answers from quiz Next Club 1

1 Real Madrid 2 Aston Villa 3 Crystal Palace 4 Monaco 5 Atletico Madrid 6 Watford 7 Zenit Saint Petersburg 8 Shanghai SIPG 9 Arsenal 10 Roma 11 Wolfsburg 12 AC Milan 13 Besiktas 14 Man Utd 15 Southampton 16 Everton 17 Southampton 18 Liverpool 19 Fenerbache 20 PSG

Winning Goals

The game of football is about scoring goals. Some are more memorable than others, especially last minute winners. Have a go at answering these theme related questions.

1. Which player scored a 90th minute goal to win the 2012/13 Europa League final?

2. Who scored the winning goal in the 2018 FA Cup final?

3. Didier Drogba scored the only goal of the 2010 FA Cup final. Who were the opponents?

4. In what year did Gianfranco Zola score the winning goal of the UEFA Cup Winners Cup?

5. Which player scored the winning goal in the 2009 FA Cup final?

6. David Webb scored Chelsea's winner in the 1970 FA Cup final. Which player took the throw in that led to his goal?

7. Which player conceded winning goals to Chelsea in both the FA Cup finals in both 2000 and 2010?

8. Frank Leboeuf scored a winning penalty vs Leicester in the 5th round of the FA Cup in 1996/97. Who won the penalty for the Blues?

9. Whose goal clinched the Premier League title for Chelsea in the 2014/15 season?

10. Who did the same thing for Chelsea in the 2016/17 season?

11. Which newly promoted team did Hernan Crespo score a last minute winner against on the opening day of the 2005/06 league season?

12. In the final home game of the 2004/05 season which player missed a last minute penalty for Chelsea before scoring from the rebound?

13. In which year did Tony Dorigo score the winning goal in the Zenith Data Systems Cup at Wembley?

14. Whose goal in the 2004/05 Champions League quarter final knocked Arsenal out of the competition?

15. Mateja Kezman scored a winning goal for Chelsea in the final of which competition?

16. Which player scored the deciding goal vs Liverpool in the 2007/08 Champions League semi-final?

17. Frank Lampard scored a winning penalty vs Stoke City in December 2009. Which future Blues keeper did he score against?

18. Who scored the winning goal vs Leicester City on his debut in August 2003?

19. Who scored all four goals in his last Chelsea appearance in a 4-3 win vs Nottingham Forest in 1961?

20. Which player scored the winning goal in his final appearance as the Blues beat FC Copenhagen in 1998 and then joined the Danish club?

Answers from quiz South America

1 Gus Poyet 2 David Luiz 3 Ramires 4 Juliano Belletti 5 Argentina 6 Juan Cuadrado 7 One 8 2013 9 Claudio Pizarro 10 Sheffield Wednesday 11 Two 12 Lucas Piazon 13 Willy Caballero 14 Oscar 15 Alexandre Pato 16 Hernan Crespo 17 Jose Mourinho 18 Derby County 19 Franco Di Santo 20 Corinthians

Who Said?

Read the quote from some in Chelsea's history. Who said the quote?

1. I am not one from the bottle, I think I am a special one.

2. I'm looking forward to seeing some sexy football.

3. I'm signing for the Champions League winner.

4. I have a go at defenders, and they have a go at me. We argue... Whatever happens on the pitch stays on the pitch.

5. When I joined the club, I came to play my part. I'm really happy to have been a part of Chelsea history.

6. If you are happy you are a geezer.

7. You can have a striker who scores 50 goals in one season but if you win nothing it means nothing.

8. I had 11 wonderful years here. I'll always class this as my home. I loved it and I'm sorry I had to leave.

9. He [Dennis Wise] could start a row in an empty house.

10. Chelsea: it's a name. It's probably the greatest name in the world: Chelsea. You think about it. What does it conjure up? It conjures up the best part of the biggest city in the world. It's magical.

11. It was obvious from the moment we arrived in Baghdad and saw soldiers carrying machine guns that leisure activities would be limited.

12. Tommy Docherty and Ron 'Chopper Harris' invented soccer violence. It's when they retired that it spread to the terraces

13. Last Thursday we received a letter dated next Monday complaining about appalling language in the Shed at today's match against Everton. You have been warned.

14. When Vinnie Jones and Mick Hartford were in the same side you'd have needed crash helmets to play against them, never mind shin pads!

15. The moment I turned up for training and saw Zola, I knew it was time to go.

16. Chelsea are the greatest club I've known. The people here have taken it on the chin for 50 years and always come up smiling. That takes some doing.

17. Wisey said I think too much but I have to do all his thinking for him.

18. I believe [Chelsea fans] are the greatest fans in world football. You have supported me from the moment I arrived.

19. I don't care – I won the World Cup.

20. If Chelsea are naive and pure then I'm Little Red Riding Hood.

Answers from quiz Winning Goals

1 Branislav Ivanovic 2 Eden Hazard 3 Portsmouth 4 1998 5 Frank Lampard 6 Ian Hutchinson 7 David James 8 Erland Johnsen 9 Eden Hazard 10 Michy Batshuayi 11 Wigan Athletic 12 Claude Makelele 13 1990 14 Wayne Bridge 15 League Cup 16 Didier Drogba 17 Asmir Begovic 18 Adrian Mutu 19 Jimmy Greaves 20 Brian Laudrup

Italy

Chelsea has been heavily influenced by Italy, especially since the 1990s. How many of these themed related questions can you get right?

1. Which Italian was the Chelsea manager when they won the Champions League in 2012?

2. In which Italian stadium did Dennis Wise score in back in 1999?

3. Who was the Blues boss when they won the 1998 UEFA Cup Winners Cup?

4. Which Italian scored the only goal in that game?

5. Jorginho signed for Chelsea from which club in 2018?

6. In which year did the Blues sign Pierluigi Casiraghi?

7. Who played in goal for Chelsea in the 2002 FA Cup final?

8. Which player did Chelsea sign on loan from Inter Milan in 2000?

9. Who were the only team that Gabriele Ambrosetti scored against for the Blues?

10. Which Italian made his Chelsea debut in a 5-0 win against Arsenal at Highbury in 1998?

11. Which manager gave Emerson Palmieri his Chelsea debut?

12. Who made his debut for the Blues in 2009 before signing for Parma in 2011?

13. Davide Zappacosta signed for Chelsea in 2017 from which club?

14. In 2004, which Italian played in goal for the Blues in the Champions League semi-final away to Monaco?

15. Samuele Dalla Bona left Chelsea in 2002 to join which club?

16. Who were the first Italian team that the Blues ever faced in a competitive match?

17. Which Italian won the 2019 Europa League final as manager with Chelsea?

18. How many seasons did Claudio Ranieri spend as the Blues boss?

19. In which year did Carlo Ancelotti become the Chelsea manager?

20. Which team did the Blues beat in the 1998 UEFA Cup Winners Cup semi-final?

Answers from quiz Who Said?

1 Jose Mourinho 2 Ruud Gullit 3 Eden Hazard 4 Diego Costa 5 Didier Drogba 6 David Luiz 7 Branislav Ivanovic 8 Dennis Wise 9 Alex Ferguson 10 Jimmy Greaves 11 Colin Pates 12 Peter Osgood 13 Ken Bates 14 Tommy Langley 15 John Spencer 16 Ted Drake 17 Gianfranco Zola 18 Frank Lampard 19 Frank Leboeuf 20 Rafa Benitez

General Knowledge 3

This round tests your Chelsea general knowledge. These are questions that most Blues fans should know but how many will you get correct?

1. Which London Borough is Stamford Bridge in?

2. What music track do Chelsea run out to just before kick off?

3. Who is the oldest person to play for the Blues?

4. What is the name of the ice hockey team that Petr Cech signed for in 2019?

5. What was the name of the children's book series written by Lampard?

6. Which Irishman played for the Blues in the 1970 FA Cup final?

7. Who was the second Chelsea player to score in the Roman Abramovich era?

8. Who was the second player to score for the Blues in an FA Cup final?

9. Which goalkeeper did Frank Lampard score more goals against than any other whilst at Chelsea?

10. Who was Chelsea's unused substitute in the 1971 Cup Winners Cup final replay?

11. Which former Chelsea player won £17,000 from a slot machine and donated it to charity?

12. Who danced to 'Men In Black' alongside Peter Shilton for Sport Relief in

2010?

13. Which former Chelsea striker was the AFCON's top goalscorer in 2006 and 2008?

14. Who refereed the 1994 FA Cup final?

15. Which Chelsea player had the nickname 'The Rock'?

16. In which year was Dave Sexton sacked as the Blues boss?

17. Who did Chelsea beat in the 1971 UEFA Cup Winners Cup quarter final?

18. How many times did Frank Lampard have to take a penalty for Chelsea vs West Ham in December 2009?

19. How many games did the Blues play in the 2012/13 season?

20. Who was the first Chelsea player to score at a World Cup?

Answers from quiz Italy

1 Roberto Di Matteo 2 San Siro 3 Gianluca Vialli 4 Gianfranco Zola 5 Napoli 6 1998 7 Carlo Cudicini 8 Christian Panucci 9 Galatasaray 10 Luca Percassi 11 Antonio Conte 12 Fabio Borini 13 Torino 14 Marco Ambrosio 15 AC Milan 16 Roma 17 Maurizio Sarri 18 Four 19 2009 20 Vicenza

Almost Impossible 1

This set of questions are as the title suggests. How many of these almost impossible questions can you get correct?

1. Who has scored the most goals for Chelsea without scoring a single penalty?

2. Who is the youngest ever player to be named in a Chelsea matchday squad?

3. Which former Chelsea player was also a member of the London Stock Exchange?

4. Which Chelsea player only had one eye?

5. Who became the first female to officiate in a major men's UEFA game when Chelsea played Liverpool in the 2019 UEFA Super Cup?

6. What was the name of the first person to win a reality show called 'Football Icon' and a contract with Chelsea as his prize?

7. What was the name of the first ever black player to sign for Chelsea?

8. Who was the composer/producer of Chelsea's 1997 FA Cup final song 'Blue Day'?

9. Which Chelsea player was the best man at Tommy Langley's wedding?

10. Who became Chelsea manager for just one day back in 1978?

11. In what year did Stamford Bridge hold its first FA Cup final?

12. Who scored an own goal in his only appearance for the Blues?

13. Who captained Chelsea in their first FA Cup final in 1915?

14. Who has played the most games for Chelsea without ever being named in the starting XI?

15. What was the original name for Fulham Broadway tube station?

16. Who was the last Chelsea player to captain England before John Terry?

17. Which Chelsea player declared bankruptcy in 2011?

18. Which Chelsea player died during World War I?

19. Who did Chelsea beat in their first FA Youth Cup final win back in 1960?

20. Which Chelsea player had an autobiography called 'The Working Mans' Ballet'?

Answers from quiz General Knowledge 3

1 Hammersmith and Fulham 2 Liquidator 3 Mark Schwarzer 4 Guildford Flames 5 Frankie's Magic Football 6 John Dempsey 7 Juan Sebastian Veron 8 Peter Houseman 9 Brad Friedel 10 Paddy Mulligan 11 Emmanuel Petit 12 Jason Cundy 13 Samuel Eto'o 14 David Elleray 15 Marcel Desailly 16 1974 17 Bruges 18 Three 19 69 20 Dan Petrescu

Jose Mourinho

Jose Mourinho was one of the most successful managers in Chelsea's history but how much do you know about him?

1. What nationality was Jose Mourinho?

2. Jose Mourinho joined Chelsea as manager in 2004 from which club?

3. Which Chelsea manager did he replace?

4. Who did Jose appoint as his Assistant Manager in 2004?

5. Which player did he announce as his first club captain?

6. How many points did Jose Mourinho win in his first Premier League season?

7. What did Mourinho do with his Premier League winners medal that he won in the 2005/06 season?

8. Jose left the Blues by mutual consent in 2007 just two days after drawing 1-1 against which club?

9. Who replaced him as manager and reached the Champions League final?

10. In 2013, Mourinho re-joined Chelsea after leaving which club?

11. Mourinho suffered his first ever home league defeat as Chelsea manager against which club?

12. Who was the first player to score under Jose Mourinho's management at Chelsea?

13. How many Premier League trophies did he win?

14. Jose Mourinho knocked the Blues out of the 2009/10 Champions League with which team?

15. In 2014, which manager did he label as a 'specialist in failure'?

16. In which position did Jose Mourinho play in during his playing career?

17. In which year did he win the Community Shield with the Blues?

18. Which team did Mourinho defeat in the 2006/07 League Cup final?

19. Which team beat him in his last ever game as Chelsea manager in 2015?

20. Who replaced him as manager after his second spell in 2015?

Answers from quiz Almost Impossible 1

1 Tommy Baldwin 2 Nathaniel Chalobah (15 years old) 3 Alfred Bower 4 Bob Thompson 5 Stephanie Frappart 6 Sam Hurrell 7 Fred Hanley 8 Mike Connaris 9 Clive Walker 10 Frank Upton 11 1920 12 John Carr 13 Jack Harrow 14 Franco Di Santo 15 Walham Green 16 Vivian Woodward 17 Celestine Babayaro 18 George Lake 19 Preston North End 20 Alan Hudson

True or False 3

Read the following questions. Just simply answer True or False for each question.

1. Gianluca Vialli lived in a castle as a child.

2. Ron Harris played for England in the 1970 World Cup.

3. Ruud Gullit played for Ajax.

4. Diego Costa was born in Brazil.

5. Chris Sutton was once named the Chelsea captain.

6. Jody Morris played over 100 games for the Blues.

7. Gustavo Poyet was Argentinian.

8. In the 2012/13 season Fernando Torres scored in seven different competitions for Chelsea.

9. Josh McEachran refused to travel to games on a plane.

10. Adrian Mutu was once banned from playing for Romania after posting a picture of Mr Bean on Facebook.

11. Diego Costa was once sent off for kicking a pitch invader.

12. Arjen Robben used to cycle to Cobham from his house when he first joined the club.

13. Steve Clarke used to play for Rangers.

14. Eidur Gudjohnsen signed for Chelsea from Bolton.

15. Mark Hughes once played for Wales and Bayern Munich in the same day.

16. Robert Fleck scored more goals against Chelsea than for them.

17. Ian Hutchinson died at the age of 31.

18. Ramires left Chelsea to play in China.

19. Micky Hazard once scored four goals in a Chelsea match.

20. In 2006 William Gallas scored an own goal whilst playing for Chelsea against Spurs.

Youth Products

Some of the club's greatest players have come through the youth system at Chelsea. How many of these youth product questions can you get right?

1. Who was the first youth team product to score 100 goals for the Blues?

2. How old was John Terry when he joined Chelsea?

3. Which youth team player initially retired at the age of 21 in 2010 before coming back and playing for the club a year later?

4. Who left the Blues in 1984 and then knocked them out of the League Cup at the semi-final a year later?

5. Where was Graeme Le Saux born?

6. Which youth team product scored in the 1997 FA Cup final for the Blues?

7. Paul Hughes scored on his Chelsea debut against which club?

8. Who scored a hattrick and an own goal in a game vs Wolves in 2019?

9. Which youth team product scored a hattrick against the Blues for Tottenham back in 1960?

10. Who was the first youth team product to become Chelsea manager?

11. Which goalkeeper made his only Blues appearance in a game vs West Ham back in 1997?

12. How many goals did Ron Harris scored for Chelsea?

13. Who won the Chelsea Player of the Year in 1993?

14. Which youth team product was named in the starting XI when the Blues won the 2018/19 Europa League final?

15. Who opened the scoring for Chelsea in the 2014/15 League Cup final?

16. Ray Wilkins left the Blues in 1979. Which club did he join?

17. How many games did John Bumstead play for Chelsea?

18. Which manager gave Bobby Tambling his debut for the Blues?

19. Which youth team product scored 43 goals for Chelsea between 1974 and 1980?

20. Which player made his Wales debut in 2017 to become the Blues youngest ever international?

Answers from quiz True or False 3

1 True 2 False 3 False 4 True 5 True 6 True 7 False 8 True 9 False 10 True 11 False 12 True 13 False 14 True 15 True 16 False 17 False 18 True 19 False 20 False

1990s Chelsea

This set of questions is all about Chelsea in the 1990s decade. How well do you know you club?

1. Who was Chelsea's first manager in the 1990s?

2. Which trophy did the Blues win at Wembley in 1990?

3. Which member of Chelsea's 1970 FA Cup winning side became the Blues manager in 1993?

4. Who were the first ever team that Chelsea played against in the Premier League?

5. Which player became the club's £2.3m record signing after moving from Watford in 1994?

6. Who played in goal for Chelsea in the 1997 FA Cup final?

7. Who scored in seven consecutive Premier League games in the 1993/94 season?

8. Which 1990s manager left Chelsea to become the England manager?

9. In 1997 Chelsea beat Tottenham 6-1 at White Hart Lane. Who scored a hattrick in that game?

10. Chelsea Director, Matthew Harding, died in a helicopter crash after watching the Blues lost to which club?

11. Which Norwegian side did Chelsea play on a snow covered pitch in 1997?

12. Chelsea won the UEFA Cup Winners Cup in 1998. Who did they defeat in the final?

13. Who scored the only goal of the game?

14. Who was the Blues first £10m signing?

15. Who were Chelsea's shirt sponsor in the 1997 FA Cup final?

16. How many Ballon d'Or winners played for the Blues in the decade?

17. In 1996, Chelsea signed Gianluca Vialli from which club?

18. Who played in goal for the Blues in the 1998 League Cup final?

19. Which Chelsea player scored against the Blues in the 1994 FA Cup final?

20. Who scored the Blues last goal before the year 2000?

Answers from quiz Youth Products

1 Jimmy Greaves 2 14 3 Sam Hutchinson 4 Clive Walker 5 Jersey 6 Eddie Newton 7 Derby County 8 Tammy Abraham 9 Bobby Smith 10 Ken Shellito 11 Nick Colgan 12 14 13 Frank Sinclair 14 Andreas Christensen 15 John Terry 16 Manchester Utd 17 409 18 Ted Drake 19 Tommy Langley 20 Ethan Ampadu

Anagrams 1

The classic game of anagrams. Rearrange the letters to reveal the names of these Chelsea related puzzles.

1. CHELSEA IS MINE
2. ACID STOOGE
3. VANILLA COUPLE
4. GRAINY DWEEB
5. CLEARLY MISLEAD
6. HALAL CAKE CLIMB
7. BETTER OPEN IT
8. SNORER DONE FART
9. LORD FUN OATMEAL
10. A NINTH CUSHION
11. INEPT VAN
12. NOT SPECIAL
13. INSIDE NEWS
14. DEAD MUFFIN
15. CREATED PUNS
16. CREAKY LOG
17. A HAUNTED MAP
18. BARNYARD RENT
19. RACKET SPORT
20. RIOT MANIACS

Defenders

A great team is built on a solid defence. Over the years the Blues have had many heroes at the back. Have a go at these defender related questions.

1. Which defender captained Chelsea in the 2019 Europa League final?

2. What country did Steve Clarke play for?

3. Which defender earned his 100th England cap whilst at Chelsea?

4. Who was David Luiz's centre back partner for the 2012 Champions League final?

5. Which defender scored a headed equaliser against Liverpool in May 2003 in the final game of the Ken Bates era?

6. Frank Sinclair represented which country at the 1998 World Cup?

7. Which Blues defender had the nickname 'Jamaica'?

8. Mario Melchiot scored in a Charity Shield match against which club in 2000?

9. Which defender had the nickname 'Chapi'?

10. Who did Chelsea sign from Aberdeen in 1984?

11. Asier Del Horno was sent off for fouling which player in a game with Barcelona in 2006?

12. Which defender wore the number 25 shirt before Gianfranco Zola?

13. Papy Djilobodji made one appearance for the Blues as a 90th minute

substitute. Who were the opponents?

14. Who scored an own goal at Stamford Bridge whilst on loan with Derby in 2018?

15. Who was the first ever player to be sent off for and against Chelsea?

16. Which defender scored a penalty against Sheffield Wednesday in 1955 in a game that guaranteed Chelsea won the league title?

17. Who was Chelsea's first ever Brazilian player?

18. Which defender scored the Blue's first ever penalty?

19. Which defender went in goal for Chelsea in 2005 after Carlo Cudicini was injured vs Newcastle?

20. Which defender made his only appearance for the Blues in a game vs Hapoel Tel Aviv in 2001?

Answers from quiz Anagrams 1

1 Michael Essien 2 Diego Costa 3 Paul Canoville 4 Wayne Bridge 5 Marcel Desailly 6 Michael Ballack 7 Peter Bonetti 8 Fernando Torres 9 Florent Malouda 10 Ian Hutchinson 11 Pat Nevin 12 Colin Pates 13 Dennis Wise 14 Damien Duff 15 Dan Petrescu 16 Gary Locke 17 Ethan Ampadu 18 Ryan Bertrand 19 Scott Parker 20 Mario Stanic

French Connection

Over the years Chelsea have had many connections with all things France. How many of these French related questions can you answer correctly?

1. Who was the first Frenchman to play for Chelsea?

2. Which defender made his Blues debut against Man Utd in 1997?

3. Who did Chelsea sign on loan from Cannes in 1998?

4. Who was the only player to score a winning goal in the Premier League against Chelsea in the 2004/05 season and later joined the Blues?

5. From which club did Claude Makelele sign from?

6. Which player scored on his Chelsea debut against Man Utd in August 2007?

7. Who captained the Blues in the 2002 FA Cup final?

8. Which striker scored in the 2019 UEFA Super Cup for Chelsea?

9. Against which team did William Gallas receive his only red card in a Chelsea shirt?

10. Loic Remy scored on his Blues debut. Who were the opponents?

11. Which midfielder won the 2018 World Cup whilst playing for the Blues?

12. In which year did Kurt Zouma sign for Chelsea?

13. Lassana Diarra left the Blues to sign for which club?

14. Didier Deschamps only scored one goal for Chelsea. Who were the opponents?

15. From which club did Chelsea sign Emmanuel Petit?

16. Which midfielder joined AC Milan on loan from the Blues in 2018?

17. In 2009, which player was banned for four months due to a breach of contract with his old club Lens in order to sign for Chelsea?

18. Which French side did the Blues face in the Champions League in 2000?

19. Which team did Chelsea face in three consecutive seasons in the Champions League between 2014 and 2016?

20. Which French side did the Blues face in the 2007/08 Champions League?

Answers from quiz Defenders

1 Cesar Azpilicueta 2 Scotland 3 Ashley Cole 4 Gary Cahill 5 Marcel Desailly 6 Jamaica 7 Paul Elliott 8 Manchester Utd 9 Albert Ferrer 10 Doug Rougvie 11 Lionel Messi 12 Terry Phelan 13 Walsall 14 Fikayo Tomori 15 David Luiz 16 Peter Sillett 17 Emerson Thome 18 Bob McRoberts 19 Glen Johnson 20 Joel Kitamirike

General Knowledge 4

This round tests your Chelsea general knowledge. These are questions that most Blues fans should know but how many will you get correct?

1. Which former Blue appeared for Luton Town in the 1994 FA Cup semi-final against Chelsea?

2. In which year did the Blues play in the Arctic circle?

3. In October 2019, which former Blue suffered a cardiac arrest on his birthday?

4. Which former striker had a TV partnership with Ian St John?

5. Who was the first person to play for Chelsea in an FA Cup final whilst on loan?

6. In which country was Ruud Gullit born?

7. Gareth Hall played international football for which country?

8. Which team knocked Chelsea out of the UEFA Cup in 2002?

9. What number was David Webb wearing when he scored the winning goal in the 1970 FA Cup final?

10. Who scored Chelsea's first goal in the 21st century?

11. In what year did Michael Ballack make his Blues debut?

12. Which team did Chelsea beat in the 2012 FA Cup semi-final?

13. Who gave Eden Hazard his debut for the Blues?

14. How many goals did Gianluca Vialli score for Chelsea?

15. Yossi Benayoun scored one goal for the Blues. Who were the opponents?

16. In which country was Jesper Gronkjaer born?

17. How many games did Petr Cech play for the Blues?

18. Who scored his only Chelsea goal in 1994 against Southampton despite playing 183 games?

19. Which team did the Blues knock out of the 1996 FA Cup in a penalty shootout?

20. What country did Eidur Gudjohnsen play international football for?

Answers from quiz French Connection

1 Frank Leboeuf 2 Bernard Lambourde 3 Laurent Charvet 4 Nicolas Anelka 5 Real Madrid 6 Florent Malouda 7 Marcel Desailly 8 Olivier Giroud 9 Fulham 10 Swansea City 11 N'Golo Kante 12 2014 13 Arsenal 14 Hertha Berlin 15 Barcelona 16 Tiemoue Bakayoko 17 Gael Kakuta 18 Marseille 19 PSG 20 Bordeaux

Adverts

Football clubs and players can be very attractive for advertisers to use in order to promote their products. Have a go at answering these commercial related questions.

1. Which player won the Champions League in 2012 and appeared in an advert for Lidl in 2018?

2. Which Chelsea player voiced the commentary for a Tango advert in 1992 that was later banned from UK TV?

3. Who starred in a McDonald's advert to promote the 1994 World Cup?

4. Which Frenchman appeared in a Pringles advert in 2010?

5. Who appeared in an advert for Turkish Airlines in 2015?

6. Which player featured in an advert for Tesco's in 2010?

7. Who starred in adverts for King of Shaves in 2006?

8. Which defender advertised Samsung phones alongside Rio Ferdinand and Kevin Bacon in 2018?

9. What sportswear company did Peter Osgood advertise in 1970?

10. Which former Blue featured alongside Pele in an advert for Subway in

2014?

11. What beauty company did Michael Ballack advertise in 2011?

12. Marcel Desailly advertised which beer during EURO 2016?

13. Which breakfast cereal did Glenn Hoddle advertise in 1998?

14. In 2001, which breakfast cereal did Dennis Wise advertise?

15. Who starred in an advert for the British Heart Foundation doing CPR to the song 'Staying Alive'?

16. Which player advertised Clarks Shoes in the 1980s?

17. Which shaving brand did Tommy Docherty advertise for?

18. Which hot beverage did Jimmy Greaves advertise whilst with Chelsea?

19. Fernando Torres made cupcakes in an advert for what company?

20. Who starred in a 2019 advert for the hair care and grooming company called Beardilizer?

1 Kerry Dixon 2 1997 3 Glenn Hoddle 4 Jimmy Greaves 5 George Weah 6 Surinam 7 Wales 8 Viking FK 9 Six 10 Tore Andre Flo 11 2006 12 Tottenham 13 Roberto Di Matteo 14 40 15 Wigan 16 Greenland 17 494 18 Erland Johnsen 19 Newcastle 20 Iceland

Next Club 2

Look at the players in this set of questions. Name the club they joined after leaving Chelsea.

1. Michael Ballack

2. Ricardo Carvalho

3. Patrick van Aanholt

4. Andriy Shevchenko

5. Carlo Cudicini

6. Wayne Bridge

7. Glen Johnson

8. Arjen Robben

9. Damien Duff

10. Robert Huth

11. William Gallas

12. Eidur Gudjohnsen

13. Hernan Crespo

14. Jesper Gronkjaer

15. Gianfranco Zola

16. Jody Morris

17. Dennis Wise

18. Tore Andre Flo

19. Chris Sutton

20. Dan Petrescu

Answers from quiz Adverts

1 Gary Cahill 2 Ray Wilkins 3 Scott Parker 4 Nicolas Anelka 5 Didier Drogba 6 Frank Lampard 7 John Terry 8 David Luiz 9 Bukta 10 Daniel Sturridge 11 L'Oreal 12 Carlsberg 13 Shredded Wheat 14 Sugar Puffs 15 Vinnie Jones 16 Kerry Dixon 17 Gillette 18 Bovril 19 Samsung 20 Olivier Giroud

Player of the Year

Just simply name the person that won the Chelsea Player of the Year in the years given in this set of questions.

1. 2000

2. 1970

3. 2012

4. 1980

5. 1981

6. 2018

7. 1995

8. 1985

9. 1978

10. 1988

11. 1976

12. 1986

13. 1994

14. 1999

15. 2007

16. 1984

17. 2008
18. 2002
19. 1991
20. 2016

Answers from quiz Next Club 2

1 Bayer Leverkusen 2 Real Madrid 3 Sunderland 4 Dynamo Kiev 5 Tottenham 6 Man City 7 Portsmouth 8 Real Madrid 9 Newcastle 10 Middlesbrough 11 Arsenal 12 Barcelona 13 Inter Milan 14 Birmingham 15 Cagliari 16 Leeds Utd 17 Leicester 18 Rangers 19 Celtic 20 Bradford City

Stamford Bridge

Stamford Bridge is the original home of Chelsea FC but how well do you know the ground? Try these questions about the Bridge.

1. In what year was Stamford Bridge first opened?
2. What is the postcode of Stamford Bridge?
3. Who owns Stamford Bridge?
4. In 1905, Middlesex lost 34-0 in a rugby match against which country?
5. In 1919, King Alphonso XIII came to watch Chelsea vs Bradford Park Avenue. Which country was the king from?
6. How many FA Cup finals has Stamford Bridge held?
7. In what year did Chelsea score their 1,000th goal at Stamford Bridge?
8. In 2003, the Stamford Bridge pitch was heavily sanded and the opposition demanded the match was replayed. Who were the opponents?
9. In 1914 Stamford Bridge hosted a match between the New York Giants and Chicago White Sox. Which sport was being played?
10. In which year did Stamford Bridge host Women's Olympiad, the first international event for women in track and field in the UK?

11. Stamford Bridge held a match between Essex and the West Indies in which sport?

12. Which American Football team was based at Stamford Bridge in 1997?

13. Which player is buried underneath the penalty spot at the Shed End?

14. The North Stand at Stamford Bridge was completed in 1994. Who was later named after?

15. What was the name of the campaign to raise money for legal costs to stop Stamford Bridge being developed into housing or a supermarket?

16. In which stand were 'The Benches' situated?

17. What was 'The Shed' known as when it was originally built?

18. In which stand can the 'Family Section' be found?

19. What is the name of the cemetery next to Stamford Bridge?

20. Chelsea's first ever game at Stamford Bridge was a friendly against which club?

Team of the 1970s

The Chelsea team of the 1970s contributed to some of the best and worst times in the club's career. How much do you know about the team of the 1970s?

1. In which year did Chelsea win the FA Cup for the first time?

2. Who did the Blues beat in the 1970 FA Cup final?

3. Who scored the winning goal?

4. On what ground did Chelsea win the 1970 FA Cup?

5. Which Chelsea player scored in every round that year?

6. The team released 'Blue is the Colour' in 1972. Which record label released it?

7. Who did Chelsea beat in the 1971 UEFA Cup Winners Cup final?

8. Peter Osgood and which other player scored in the replay?

9. Who did the Blues beat 21-0 on aggregate in the 1971/72 Cup Winners Cup?

10. Who knocked Chelsea out of the competition in the next round?

11. In which season did Chelsea get relegated into Division Two?

12. How many managers took charge of the Blues in the decade?

13. Chelsea's fastest ever goal came after just 12 seconds in a game vs Middlesbrough in 1970. Who was the goalscorer?

14. Who played in goal for Chelsea vs Ipswich on 27th December 1971?

15. In 1974, the Blues played in the first ever top flight match on a Sunday. Who were the opponents?

16. In 1977, which Chelsea player became the first ever to receive a red card for the club?

17. In what year did Chelsea first use an electronic scoreboard?

18. Which 1970 FA Cup final winning player died in car crash in 1977?

19. Which stand at Stamford Bridge was opened for the first time in 1974?

20. Peter Osgood left Chelsea in 1974. Which club did he sign for?

Answers from quiz Stamford Bridge

1 1877 2 SW6 1HS 3 Chelsea Pitch Owners plc 4 New Zealand 5 Spain 6 Three 7 1933 8 Charlton Athletic 9 Baseball 10 1924 11 Cricket 12 London Monarchs 13 Peter Osgood 14 Matthew Harding 15 Save The Bridge 16 The West Stand 17 Fulham Road End 18 The East Stand 19 Brompton Cemetery 20 Liverpool

True or False 4

Read the following questions. Just simply answer True or False for each question.

1. Ashley Cole missed two weeks of the 2008/09 season after injuring himself whilst playing a games console.

2. Gary Locke became a locksmith after he retired from football.

3. Mario Melchiot was once part of a music band with Benni McCarthy.

4. Former Blues goalkeeper Jim Molyneux also played for Wolverhampton Wanderers.

5. Craig Burley had two false front teeth.

6. Pat Nevin wrote for the NME music magazine.

7. Chelsea's tough tackling Stan Willemse had a phobia of dogs.

8. Nils Middelboe didn't have to travel to away games so he could work in a bank.

9. Dennis Wise ended his playing career with Millwall.

10. Wayne Bridge's middle name was Stamford.

11. After retiring, John Dempsey worked with people with learning disabilities.

12. Andy Townsend won the FA Cup with Aston Villa.

13. Jakob Kjeldbjerg has been the host of a Danish version of the TV show Gladiators.

14. In 2001 Andy Myers fought Michael Duberry in a charity boxing match.

15. Ray Wilkins was arrested for drink driving.

16. David Hopkin had ginger hair.

17. In 2008 Dave Beasant appeared in a celebrity version of Total Wipeout.

18. Kevin Hitchcock's son Tom was a goalkeeper for QPR.

19. Eden Hazard's mum was a women's professional footballer.

20. Mal Donaghy represented the Republic of Ireland at international level.

Answers from quiz Team of the 1970s

1 1970 2 Leeds Utd 3 David Webb 4 Old Trafford 5 Peter Osgood 6 Penny Farthing Records 7 Real Madrid 8 John Dempsey 9 Jeunesse Hautcharage 10 Atvidabergs 11 1974/75 12 Six 13 Keith Weller 14 David Webb 15 Stoke City 16 Graham Wilkins 17 1979 18 Peter Houseman 19 The East Stand 20 Southampton

Liverpool

Liverpool are one of Chelsea's biggest rivals and there have been some classic encounters between the two clubs. Have a go at answering these themed questions.

1. In which year did Chelsea first play Liverpool?

2. Who was the first person to manage both Chelsea and Liverpool?

3. Which Liverpool player slipped to allow Demba Ba to score in 2014?

4. Chelsea beat Liverpool 4-2 in the 1997 FA Cup 4th round. Who came on at half time and scored for the Blues?

5. Which player moved from Liverpool to Chelsea for £50m in 2011?

6. Who scored the first goal in the 2012 FA Cup final between Chelsea and Liverpool?

7. Which player scored twice against Liverpool for Chelsea in the 1977/78 FA Cup third round?

8. The Blues beat Liverpool in the 2005 League Cup final. Which stadium was it played in?

9. Who scored the 'Ghost Goal' against Chelsea in 2005?

10. Which player scored an own goal in the 2008 Champions League semi-final between the two clubs?

11. Who joined Liverpool from Chelsea in 1987 and later returned back to the Blues in 1992?

12. Which player scored for and against Liverpool for Chelsea in a Premier League game in 1994?

13. Who won the Chelsea Player of the Year in 1983 and also played for Liverpool?

14. Which player bit Branislav Ivanovic in a game between the two sides in 2013?

15. Who scored an emotional penalty for Chelsea against Liverpool in 2008 after his mother had recently passed away?

16. Which Israeli international played for both Chelsea and Liverpool?

17. Who ended Paul Elliott's football career after a horror challenge in 1992?

18. Which Chelsea player had a penalty saved in the 2019 UEFA Super Cup shootout?

19. Who scored the winning goal vs Liverpool in the final game of the

2002/03 season?

20. Which player has won the Champions League with both clubs despite being an unused substitute in both games?

Answers from quiz True or False 4

1 False 2 False 3 True 4 False 5 True 6 True 7 False 8 True 9 False 10 False 11 True 12 False 13 True 14 False 15 True 16 True 17 False 18 True 19 True 20 False

Dennis Wise

Dennis Wise is a Chelsea legend (and my all-time favourite player). How much do you know about Wisey?

1. From which club did Chelsea sign Dennis Wise from?

2. How many appearances did he make for Chelsea?

3. Against which side did he make his debut?

4. Against which team did he score his first Chelsea goal?

5. How many times was Dennis Wise sent off during his Blues career?

6. Who wore the number 11 shirt for Chelsea after Dennis Wise?

7. In which year did he first win the Chelsea Player of the Year?

8. In 1993 he captained the Blues for the first time. Who were the opponents?

9. How many FA Cup finals did he appear in during his entire playing career?

10. Which manager briefly stripped him of the captaincy after an incident with a taxi driver?

11. In which year did Dennis Wise score against AC Milan in the San Siro?

12. In 2017, he competed in 'I'm a Celebrity... Get Me Out Of Here'. What position did he finish?

13. Dennis Wise scored in his final game Chelsea. Who were the opponents?

14. Which club did he sign for after leaving Chelsea?

15. He scored the only goal on his England debut in 1991. Who were the opponents?

16. After retiring he managed Millwall, Leeds Utd and which other club?

17. Which Chelsea player did he appoint as his Assistant Manager?

18. Wise also became an Executive Director of which club?

19. He captained Chelsea to a UEFA Super Cup win in 1998. Who were the opponents?

20. What initiation did he introduce that still happens to new players now?

Answers from quiz Liverpool
1 1907 2 Rafa Benitez 3 Steven Gerrard 4 Mark Hughes 5 Fernando Torres 6 Ramires 7 Clive Walker 8 The Millennium Stadium 9 Luis Garcia 10 John Arne Riise 11 Nigel Spackman 12 Craig Burley 13 Joey Jones 14 Luis Suarez 15 Frank Lampard 16 Yossi Benayoun 17 Dean Saunders 18 Tammy Abraham 19 Jesper Gronkjaer 20 Daniel Sturridge

1980s Chelsea

This set of questions is all about Chelsea in the 1980s decade. How well do you know you club?

1. In which division were Chelsea playing in at the start of the decade?

2. How many times were the Blues promoted in the 1980s?

3. In 1980 Ron Harris made his 795th and final appearance for Chelsea. Who were the opponents?

4. In which year did Paul Canoville make his Chelsea debut, making him the club's first ever black player?

5. Chelsea started the 1984/85 back in Division One. Who scored a famous goal against Arsenal on the opening day?

6. In the same season Chelsea reached the League Cup semi-final. Who knocked them out?

7. Which manager signed Kerry Dixon, Pat Nevin and Nigel Spackman?

8. Who replaced him as the Blues boss in 1985?

9. In what year did Chelsea first have a shirt sponsor?

10. Which company was on the shirt?

11. In 1983 Chelsea survived relegation from Division Two by beating Bolton in May. Who scored the only goal of the game?

12. Who did Chelsea beat Man City in the 1986 Full Members Cup final.

What was the score?

13. Who scored a hattrick in this game?

14. Which Chelsea youth product made front page news after being stabbed by a group of Millwall fans in 1984?

15. Who played the most games for the Blues in the decade?

16. How many points did Chelsea finish with at the end of the 1988/89 season?

17. In March 1986 Chelsea played a friendly in which international country?

18. Before becoming Chelsea Chairman in 1982, which club did Ken Bates leave as Vice Chairman?

19. Graham Roberts joined the Blues from which club?

20. How many penalties did he score for Chelsea in the 1988/89 season?

Answers from quiz Dennis Wise

1 Wimbledon 2 445 3 Derby County 4 Sunderland 5 8 6 Boudewijn Zenden 7 1998 8 Wimbledon 9 Five 10 Glenn Hoddle 11 1999 12 6th 13 Manchester City 14 Leicester City 15 Turkey 16 Swindon Town 17 Gus Poyet 18 Newcastle Utd 19 Real Madrid 20 Sing a song in front of everyone

Away Kits

Blue is definitely the colour where Chelsea are concerned but these questions are to test your knowledge of the club's away kits.

1. What were the two main official colours of Chelsea's 1994/95 away kit?

2. What colour away shirt did the Blues wear in the 2008/09 FA Cup final?

3. In 1997, whose away kit were Chelsea forced to wear after the referee decided the two teams' shirts clashed?

4. In 1986, Chelsea wore a green away kit. What was the name of the shade of green?

5. The Blues wore a one-time only shirt in 1966 for an FA Cup semi-final. What two colours were the stripes?

6. Between 1992 and 1994 Chelsea wore a white away shirt with which colour pinstripes?

7. In what year did the Blues first have an all-black away kit?

8. What colour kit did Chelsea wear in the 1986 Full Members Cup final?

9. In which season was the 'Castrol GTX' shirt first worn?

10. What was the first shirt sponsor to appear on a Chelsea away kit?

11. In which season did Commodore Amiga first appear on a Chelsea away kit?

12. Other than black, which colour featured on the 2010/11 away kit?

13. What colour wear the shorts for the 2004/05 season away kit?

14. What colour away shirt did Chelsea wear when they played in the Cup Winners Cup semi-final at Stamford Bridge in 1998?

15. How many Premier League goals did Andriy Shevchenko score wearing an away kit?

16. What colour away kit was Didier Drogba wearing when he scored a Champions League hattrick for Chelsea?

17. What three main colours appeared on Chelsea's shirt for their visit to the Nou Camp in 2012?

18. What shape made up the red and white away shirt between 1992 and 1994?

19. Between 1991 and 1993 Chelsea produced a yellow away kit that resembled a graph. What colour was the graph line?

20. What colour shirt did Gianfranco Zola wear on his Chelsea debut?

Answers from quiz 1980s Chelsea

1 Division Two 2 Two 3 Oldham Athletic 4 1982 5 Kerry Dixon 6 Sunderland 7 John Neal 8 John Hollins 9 1983 10 Gulf Air 11 Clive Walker 12 5-4 13 David Speedie 14 Robert Isaac 15 Colin Pates 16 99 17 Iraq 18 Wigan

General Knowledge 5

This round tests your Chelsea general knowledge. These are questions that most Blues fans should know but how many will you get correct?

1. Which Chelsea player was sent off in the 2012 FIFA World Club Cup final?

2. In what year did Frank Sinclair makes his debut for the Blues?

3. In what country did Chelsea play the Turkish club Besiktas in a 2003 Champions League away game?

4. Which club did Michael Duberry join after leaving the Blues in 1999?

5. How many goals did David Speedie score for Chelsea?

6. Who was the Blues manager when they lost to Tottenham in the 2008 League Cup final?

7. In what year did Ricardo Carvalho make his final appearance for Chelsea?

8. Who played in 164 consecutive league games for the Blues between 2001 and 2005?

9. Claudio Ranieri left Chelsea to manage which club in 2004?

10. What squad number was Michael Essien given when he joined the Blues in 2005?

11. Which country did Andy Townsend play for?

12. In what year did Micky Droy make his Blues debut?

13. Who wore the number 11 shirt for Chelsea in the 1993/94 season?

14. Which animal invaded the pitch in a game between Chelsea and Liverpool at Anfield in 1987?

15. Who did the Blues compete against in their first ever penalty shootout?

16. Which Chelsea player bleached his hair during the 1998 World Cup?

17. In which year did the Blues first play QPR?

18. Which national team did Chelsea play at Stamford Bridge in 1979?

19. What was the first trophy Joe Cole won as a player?

20. Which club did Wayne Bridge join on loan in 2006 whilst at Chelsea?

Answers from quiz Away Kits

1 Tangerine and Graphite 2 Yellow 3 Coventry City 4 Jade 5 Blue and black 6 Red 7 2002 8 White 9 1974/75 10 Gulf Air 11 1993 12 Orange 13 Grey 14 Yellow 15 Zero 16 White 17 White, black and yellow 18 Diamond 19 Blue 20 Yellow

Holland

There have been many connections between Chelsea and Holland. How many of these Dutch related questions can you get correct?

1. Which Dutchman was Chelsea manager when they won the 1997 FA Cup?

2. Who was the first Dutchman to play for the Blues?

3. Which goalkeeper was named in Chelsea's starting line-up for the 1998 League Cup final?

4. Arjen Robben signed for Chelsea from which club?

5. In which year did Mario Melchiot make his Chelsea debut?

6. Which Dutchman came on as a sub for Chelsea in the 2002 FA Cup final?

7. Which defender was sent off against Arsenal in May 2007?

8. Patrick van Aanholt scored one goal for Chelsea. Who were the opponents?

9. Which manager gave Nathan Ake his debut for the Blues?

10. How many hattricks did Jimmy Floyd Hasselbaink score for Chelsea?

11. Ian Maatsen made his Blues debut against which team?

12. In which year did Jeffrey Bruma make his Chelsea debut?

13. Which manager signed Marco van Ginkel from Vitesse?

14. Nathan Ake joined which club after leaving Chelsea in 2017?

15. Who were the first Dutch side to play Chelsea in a competitive match?

16. Which Dutchman won the 2009 FA Cup as Chelsea manager?

17. In which year did the Blues first face a Dutch side in the Champions League?

18. In which city did Chelsea win the 2013 Europa League final?

19. Which former Manchester Utd player was sent off for Ajax against the Blues in 2019?

20. Who scored a hattrick against Chelsea for Arsenal in 2011?

1 Gary Cahill 2 1991 3 Germany 4 Leeds Utd 5 64 6 Avram Grant 7 2010 8 Frank Lampard 9 Valencia 10 Five 11 Republic of Ireland 12 1971 13 Dennis Wise 14 A dog 15 Leicester City 16 Dan Petrescu 17 1968 18 China 19 League Cup 20 Fulham

Nicknames

Chelsea have had many nicknames over the years as have many players. Who do these Chelsea nicknames belong to?

1. Special One
2. Chopper
3. Butch
4. Rambo
5. Sideshow Bob
6. Dave
7. Rodney Trotter
8. El Nino
9. The Bison
10. Johnny Bravo
11. Tin Tin
12. The African Zidane
13. Gatling Gun
14. Berge
15. Mulder
16. The Cat
17. Le Sulk
18. Windmill

19. Flasher

20. Sponge

Answers from quiz Holland

1 Ruud Gullit 2 Ken Monkou 3 Ed De Goey 4 PSV 5 2000 6 Boudewijn Zenden 7 Khalid Boulahrouz 8 Newcastle 9 Rafa Benitez 10 Three 11 Grimsby Town 12 2009 13 Jose Mourinho 14 Bournemouth 15 DWS Amsterdam 16 Guus Hiddink 17 1999 18 Amsterdam 19 Daley Blind 20 Robin van Persie

Previous Club 2

Look at the players in this set of questions. From which club did Chelsea sign them from?

1. Eden Hazard

2. Ashley Cole

3. Petr Cech

4. Michael Ballack

5. Ricardo Carvalho

6. Andriy Shevchenko

7. Claude Makelele

8. Hernan Crespo

9. Gianfranco Zola

10. Michael Essien

11. Joe Cole

12. Gary Cahill

13. Gianluca Vialli

14. Roberto Di Matteo

15. Ruud Gullit

16. Mark Hughes

17. Frank Leboeuf

18. Jimmy Floyd Hasselbaink

19. Dan Petrescu

20. Branislav Ivanovic

Answers from quiz Nicknames

1 Jose Mourinho 2 Ron Harris 3 Ray Wilkins 4 Ramires 5 David Luiz 6 Cesar Azpilicueta 7 David Lee 8 Fernando Torres 9 Michael Essien 10 Andre Schurrle 11 Kevin De Bruyne 12 John Mikel Obi 13 George Hilsdon 14 Graeme Le Saux 15 Dan Petrescu 16 Peter Bonetti 17 Nicolas Anelka 18 Ian Hutchinson 19 Clive Walker 20 Tommy Baldwin

Substitutes

Substitutes can change a game, for better or worse. How many of these sub related questions can you get right?

1. In what year did Chelsea make their first ever substitute in a competitive game?

2. Who became the first person to make 50 sub appearances for the Blues?

3. Who became the first person to make 100 sub appearances for Chelsea?

4. Which player made a sub appearance in the 1997 FA Cup final?

5. Who became Chelsea's first ever sub to be sent off in a match?

6. Who became the club's first ever substitute to score an own goal?

7. In 1994 which Chelsea substitute scored and was later sent off in a game vs Sheffield Wednesday?

8. Which player was sent off for the Blues as a substitute in the 2006/07 League Cup final?

9. In 1997, Mark Hughes came on as a sub against Liverpool in a dramatic

comeback in the FA Cup. Who did he replace at half time?

10. Which player came on as a substitute for Chelsea in the 1970 FA Cup final and the replay?

11. Who came on as a half time substitute in 1985 vs Sheffield Wednesday and scored within 15 seconds?

12. In what year did Peter Houseman become the Blues first ever 'Super Sub'?

13. Gianfranco Zola was a super sub in the 1997/98 Cup Winners Cup final. Who did he replace?

14. Which player threw his Chelsea shirt to the ground after being substituted in a match with Southampton in 1993?

15. In 2006, which winger came on as a sub vs Liverpool and was subbed off just five minutes later?

16. In 1980, who became the first Chelsea player to score on his debut as a substitute?

17. How many substitutions did the Blues make in the 2013 Europa League final?

18. In 1992, who became the first Chelsea substitute to be substituted?

19. Which substitute scored in the final minute of the 2012 Champions League semi-final at the Nou Camp?

20. In what minute what John Terry substituted off in his final game for Chelsea in 2017?

Answers from quiz Previous Club 2

1 Lille 2 Arsenal 3 Rennes 4 Bayern Munich 5 Porto 6 AC Milan 7 Real Madrid 8 Inter Milan 9 Parma 10 Lyon 11 West Ham 12 Bolton 13 Juventus 14 Lazio 15 Sampdoria 16 Man Utd 17 Stratsbourg 18 Atletico Madrid 19 Sheffield Wednesday 20 Lokomotiv Moscow

Bad Boys

Football is known as the beautiful game but how many of these Chelsea bad boy questions can you answer correctly?

1. Adrian Mutu and Mark Bosnich were both sacked from Chelsea for taking what substance?

2. Which player was given an 18 month jail sentence for passing on counterfeit £10 notes?

3. Who was given a nine month prison sentence after a pub assault in 2015?

4. Medi Abalimba was sent to prison for 4 years after impersonating which Chelsea footballer?

5. Which Chelsea player was sacked after letting off a smoke bomb in a dressing room?

6. Which former striker handed himself into the police after admitting to a sexual offence whilst driving in 2019?

7. In 1965 several Chelsea players were sent home for breaking a curfew. Which town were they sent home from?

8. Tommy Docherty resigned as the Blues boss after a fracas during pre-season in which country?

9. Kepa Arrizabalaga refused to be substituted during a League Cup final in 2019. Who was set to replace him?

10. Which Chelsea player was stripped of the captaincy after being charged

of assault and criminal damage involving a taxi driver in 1995?

11. In 1992, Vinnie Jones released a video that caused major uproar with the FA. What was the video called?

12. Eden Hazard was sent off for kicking a ball boy during a League Cup semi-final. Who were the opponents?

13. John Terry was banned by the FA after being accused of racially abusing an opponent. Who was the opponent?

14. Which Chelsea player accidently shot a student with an air rifle in 2011?

15. In 2001, six Chelsea players refused to travel with the squad for an away game in the UEFA Cup. Which country were Chelsea playing in?

16. In 2007, which Blues boss spent a night in prison after an altercation involving his dog?

17. Which Chelsea player dropped his shorts as part of a goal celebration in 1997?

18. Who was sent off for Chelsea on his debut in 1982?

19. In 1977, which Chelsea player scored an own goal and got sent off in the same game?

20. How many times was Dennis Wise sent off during the 1998/99 season?

Answers from quiz Substitutes

1 1965 2 Tore Andre Flo 3 Salomon Kalou 4 Gianluca Vialli 5 Steve Clarke 6 Michael Duberry 7 David Lee 8 John Mikel Obi 9 Scott Minto 10 Marvin Hinton 11 Paul Canoville 12 1966 13 Tore Andre Flo 14 Graeme Le Saux 15 Damien Duff 16 Chris Hutchings 17 Zero 18 Joe Allon 19 Fernando Torres 20 26th

Eden Hazard

Eden Hazard was one of the most gifted players to ever appear in a Chelsea shirt. Try to answer these questions related to him.

1. What nationality was Eden Hazard?

2. How many appearances did he make for Chelsea?

3. Against which side did he make his debut?

4. How many goals did he score for the Blues?

5. What shirt number did he originally wear at Chelsea?

6. Hazard was later given the number 10 shirt. Who was given that number after he left the club?

7. In which year did he first win the Chelsea Player of the Year?

8. Hazard won the Chelsea Goal of the Season three times. Who did he score against to win it in the 2015/16 season?

9. Against which team did he score his first Chelsea goal?

10. How many Premier League trophies did he win?

11. Eden Hazard captained Belgium in the 2018 World Cup. In which position did they finish?

12. How many times did he captain Chelsea?

13. What trophy did he win in his final game for Chelsea?

14. Which club did he sign for after leaving Chelsea?

15. Hazard also had two brothers that signed for Chelsea. Kylian was one but who was the other?

16. Who came on as a substitute for Hazard in the 2012 World Club Cup final?

17. Which Chelsea player did he play alongside at Lille before moving to the Blues?

18. Hazard scored Chelsea hattricks against Newcastle and which other club?

19. In 2017, Eden Hazard became part owner of which North American Soccer League franchise?

20. Which other Chelsea player also part owned the club?

Answers from quiz Bad Boys

1 Cocaine 2 Mickey Thomas 3 Kerry Dixon 4 Gael Kakuta 5 Jacob Mellis 6 Neil Shipperley 7 Blackpool 8 Bermuda 9 Willy Caballero 10 Dennis Wise 11 Soccer's Hard Men 12 Swansea City 13 Anton Ferdinand 14 Ashley Cole 15 Israel 16 Jose Mourinho 17 Frank Sinclair 18 Joey Jones 19 Graham Wilkins 20 Three

1970s Chelsea

This set of questions is all about Chelsea in the 1970s decade. How well do you know you club?

1. Chelsea won the FA Cup in 1970. Who did they beat in the final?

2. Who was the Blues manager?

3. The game went to a replay. Where was it played?

4. Who scored the winning goal for the Blues in the replay?

5. The Blues also won the 1971 Cup Winners Cup. In which country did the final take place?

6. Who scored the first goal in the replay?

7. Bobby Tambling made his final Chelsea appearance in 1970. Which club did he join?

8. In 1975 Peter Bonetti left Chelsea to join which North American club?

9. Which country did Charlie Cooke play for?

10. Who did Chelsea lose to in the 1972 League Cup final?

11. Peter Osgood won the FA Cup with Chelsea and which other team?

12. Ray Wilkins made his Blues debut in 1973. At what age was he

appointed Chelsea captain?

13. In 1979 he left the club after they were relegated. Which club did he join?

14. In 1977 the Minister for Sport, Denis Howell, banned Chelsea fans from doing what?

15. In 1972 which Hollywood actress, accompanied by Jimmy Hill, came to watch Chelsea?

16. Peter Osgood was awarded the BBC's Goal of the Season award in 1973. Which team did he score against?

17. David Webb started in goal for Chelsea in 1972. Who were the opponents?

18. In which year did the new East Stand open?

19. How many managers did Chelsea have in the 1974/75 season?

20. Which team did Chelsea play more games against than any other in the decade?

Answers from quiz Eden Hazard

1 Belgian 2 352 3 Manchester City 4 110 5 17 6 Willian 7 2014 8 Tottenham 9 Newcastle Utd 10 Two 11 Third 12 Zero 13 Europa League 14 Real Madrid 15 Thorgan 16 Marko Marin 17 Joe Cole 18 Cardiff City 19 San Diego 1904 FC 20 Demba Ba

Hattricks

Goals can be hard to come by and so can hattricks. How many of these match ball winning related questions can you get correct?

1. Who scored a hattrick for Chelsea in the 1986 Full Members Cup final?

2. Which future Blue scored a hattrick against the Blues in the 2012 UEFA Super Cup final?

3. Didier Drogba scored a Champions League hattrick for Chelsea against Levski Sofia in which country?

4. In 1971, Peter Osgood and which other player scored a hattrick against Jeunesse Hautcharage?

5. Who scored Chelsea's first ever hattrick in the Premier League?

6. In August 1997, Gianluca Vialli scored four goals against which newly promoted side?

7. Which player scored five goals for the Blues against Walsall in 1989?

8. George Hilsdon scored a double hattrick for Chelsea in 1908 against which side?

9. Who scored a first half hattrick for the Blues against MK Dons in 2016?

10. Which player netted three times in Ray Wilkins' only game as Chelsea boss in 2009?

11. Who scored a hattrick as a substitute on his birthday in 2004?

12. Eidur Gudjohnsen only scored one hattrick for Chelsea. Who were the opponents?

13. How many hattricks did Frank Lampard scored during his Blues career?

14. Who scored a hattrick against Chelsea in the opening game of the 1997/98 Premier League season?

15. In 1986, which team had two players score a hattrick each against the Blues in the same match?

16. Who scored a hattrick for Chelsea against Roma in 1965?

17. In 2010, the Blues beat Stoke City 7-0. Which player scored a hattrick in the game?

18. Which team did Gianfranco Zola score his only Chelsea hattrick against?

19. Who scored a hattrick for the Blues in the 1999/2000 FA Cup 3rd round against Hull City?

20. Who scored a fifteen minute hattrick for Arsenal to beat Chelsea 3-2 in 1999?

1 Leeds Utd 2 Dave Sexton 3 Old Trafford 4 David Webb 5 Greece 6 John Dempsey 7 Crystal Palace 8 St. Louis Stars 9 Scotland 10 Stoke City 11 Southampton 12 18 13 Manchester Utd 14 Attending away matches 15 Raquel Welch 16 Arsenal 17 Ipswich Town 18 1974 19 Three 20 Arsenal

John Terry

John Terry was one of the most successful players and captains in the club's history. How many of these JT questions can you answer correctly?

1. How many appearances did John Terry make for Chelsea?

2. How old was John Terry when he made his Chelsea debut?

3. Against which side did he make his debut?

4. Which club did John Terry join on loan in the 1999/2000 season?

5. Who wore the number 26 shirt for Chelsea before John Terry?

6. In which year did he first win the Chelsea Player of the Year?

7. In 2001 he captained the Blues for the first time. Who were the opponents?

8. Against which team did he score his first Chelsea goal?

9. How many Premier League trophies did he win?

10. In the 2007 League Cup final Terry was stretchered off. Which player had kicked him in the face in an attempt to clear the ball?

11. In the 2008 Champions League final John Terry missed a penalty in the shootout. Who was the goalkeeper?

12. In the 2012 Champions League semi-final he was given a red card for an off the ball challenge against who?

13. John Terry made his final appearance for the Blues in 2017. Who were the opponents?

14. Which club did he sign for after leaving Chelsea?

15. In which year did Terry make his international debut?

16. Who were the opponents?

17. Which England manager named Terry as his international captain?

18. What was the name of John Terry's footballing brother?

19. What is the name of the swimwear company that he co-owns?

20. Terry only scored in one competitive England match. Who were the opponents?

Answers from quiz Hattricks

1 David Speedie 2 Radamel Falcao 3 Bulgaria 4 Tommy Baldwin 5 Gavin Peacock 6 Barnsley 7 Gordon Durie 8 Worksop Town 9 Oscar 10 Nicolas Anelka 11 Jimmy Floyd Hasselbaink 12 Blackburn Rovers 13 Five 14 Dion Dublin 15 Nottingham Forest 16 Terry Venables 17 Salomon Kalou 18 Derby County 19 Gustavo Poyet 20 Nwankwo Kanu

Midfielders

Games are won and lost in midfield but how well do you know the midfielders of Chelsea's past?

1. Which midfielder scored a fantastic chip for Chelsea at the Nou Camp in 2012?

2. Who captained the Blues in the 2000 FA Cup final?

3. In which year did Frank Lampard make his Chelsea debut?

4. Frank Lampard made over 500 appearances for the club but who was the first midfielder to do this?

5. In 2018, which midfielder became the first Englishman to score a hattrick for Chelsea in Europe since Peter Osgood?

6. Claude Makelele scored two goals for the Blues. One was against Charlton

but who were the other team?

7. Chelsea signed Nemanja Matic from Benfica in 2014 but who did he originally sign from in 2009?

8. Which World Cup winning midfielder retired at Chelsea in 2004?

9. What squad number did Steve Sidwell wear during his time with the Blues?

10. Which midfielder was sometimes known as the 'Italian Ryan Giggs'?

11. Who scored the first Premier League goal for Chelsea in the Roman Abramovich era?

12. Which midfielder scored a penalty for Bayern Munich against the Blues in 2005 and later signed for Chelsea in 2006?

13. From which club did Chelsea sign Cesc Fabregas?

14. Which player scored twice in the 1986 Full Members Cup final?

15. Oscar made over 200 appearances for the Blues. Which country did he represent?

16. Which midfielder, born in Chelsea, missed the 1970 FA Cup final through injury?

17. In what year did Roberto Di Matteo suffer a career ending injury whilst playing the for Blues?

18. Which midfielder was unbeaten in his first 100 games at Stamford Bridge?

19. How many red cards did Vinnie Jones receive during his Chelsea career?

20. Which midfielder was an Assistant manager at Chelsea under Gianluca Vialli, Luiz Felipe Scolari and Guus Hiddink?

Answers from quiz John Terry

1 717 2 17 3 Aston Villa 4 Nottingham Forest 5 Laurent Charvet 6 2001 7 Charlton Athletic 8 Gillingham 9 Five 10 Abou Diaby 11 Edwin van der Sar 12 Alexis Sanchez 13 Sunderland 14 Aston Villa 15 2003 16 Serbia & Montenegro 17 Steve McClaren 18 Paul Terry 19 Thomas Royall 20 Ukraine

Other Than Football

Sometimes clubs, players and managers branch out into things other than football. Have a go at answering these theme related questions.

1. What was Stamford Bridge originally used for when it was built in 1877?

2. After retiring from football, what other sport did Petr Cech play?

3. In 1921, Ben Howard Baker set a British record in which sport?

4. In 1920, Max Woosnam won Olympic gold in which event?

5. As well as football, what other sport was played as part of Peter Bonetti's testimonial in 1971?

6. In 1997, Clive Allen signed for the London Monarchs. What sport did they play?

7. After retiring from football, George Weah became the President of which country?

8. The club's hit song 'Blue is the Colour' peaked at what position in the UK music charts?

9. Which former Chelsea player has been in an Oscar winning movie?

10. Which former Blue appeared on the UK version of the X Factor?

11. Which Chelsea player appeared on the UK quiz show Eggheads?

12. Who came 5th in the 2016 UK version of I'm a Celebrity?

13. In 2010, which former Chelsea player had a hit with 'If I Can Dream'?

14. Which player appeared in an advert for Alaska Air?

15. Which former player moved to Canada and became a Pastor?

16. After retiring, what type of shop did Ken Monkou open in Holland?

17. Which Chelsea player competed as a professional golfer in 2002?

18. Which former Chelsea player who won an episode of the UK quiz show The Weakest Link?

19. Which former Blue scooped £5.5m on the UK National Lottery in 2015?

20. Which Chelsea player co-owned a racehorse called Crying Lightning with Joey Barton?

Answers from quiz Midfielders

1 Ramires 2 Dennis Wise 3 2001 4 John Hollins 5 Ruben Loftus-Cheek 6 Tottenham 7 Kosice 8 Emmanuel Petit 9 Nine 10 Gabriele Ambrosetti 11 Juan Sebastian Veron 12 Michael Ballack 13 Barcelona 14 Colin Lee 15 Brazil 16 Alan Hudson 17 2000 18 Michael Essien 19 None 20 Ray Wilkins

True or False 5

Read the following questions. Just simply answer True or False for each question.

1. Chelsea's first international friendly match was in Denmark in 1906.

2. Jackie Crawford played over 300 games for the Blues.

3. Chelsea manager Bobby Gould lost every that he took charge of the Blues.

4. David Speedie once advertised for Speedo swimwear.

5. Petar Borota played for Yugoslavia at the 1990 FIFA World Cup.

6. Hughie Gallacher died when he was hit by a train.

7. Paul Parker only played once for Chelsea.

8. Harry Medhurst's son was also a physio for the Blues.

9. Derek Saunders won the league with Chelsea in 1955.

10. Stamford the Lion ran the London Marathon in 2010.

11. Chelsea manager Bobby Campbell is buried in a cemetery next to Stamford Bridge.

12. Ian Britton played over 100 games in goal for the Blues.

13. Paul Canoville was homeless and spent time in prison before joining Chelsea.

14. Colin Pates used to play for Arsenal.

15. Chelsea forward Buchanan Sharp invented the electric razor in 1931.

16. In 1915 Harold Halse was the first ever person to play in three FA Cup finals for three different teams.

17. Keith Dublin was born in Ireland.

18. Mickey Thomas used to sleep in the changing rooms at Stamford Bridge overnight.

19. Chelsea youth product Mark Nicholls was a regular member of the Eastenders cast in the 1990s.

20. Steve Sidwell had his wedding vows tattooed on his back.

What's in a Name?

All of these questions are name related. How many of them can you get correct?

1. What is Kurt Zouma's middle name?

2. What is Joe Allon's middle name?

3. Whose middle name is Hycieth?

4. What is Tammy Abraham's real first name?

5. What is Mark Hughes's real first name?

6. What is Jimmy Floyd Hasselbaink's real first name?

7. Which Chelsea player's real name is Carlos Luciano da Silva?

8. What is the name of Peter Osgood's widow?

9. What was Ruud Gullit's birthname?

10. Which of Chelsea's rivals were originally named 'Dial Square'?

11. Which member of England's 1966 World Cup winning team had 'Chelsea' as a middle name?

12. In 2000, Dennis Wise took his son up with him to collect the FA Cup. What was the name of his son?

13. In the 2019 UEFA Super Cup final, which Chelsea had his name printed incorrectly on the back of his shirt?

14. Who became the first Chelsea player to have a two-letter surname?

15. How many Blues players have had 'Smith' as their surname?

16. Who was the first person to play for Chelsea with a hyphen in his name?

17. What was the name of Roman Abramovich's 533ft Super Yacht built in 2009?

18. Which Chelsea player was awarded an MBE in 1998 and an OBE in 2004?

19. Which Blues manager was Knighted in 1998?

20. What was the name of the official Chelsea matchday programme when it began in 1905?

Answers from quiz True or False 5

1 True 2 True 3 True 4 False 5 False 6 True 7 False 8 True 9 True 10 True 11 True 12 False 13 True 14 True 15 False 16 True 17 False 18 True 19 False 20 True

Tottenham

Tottenham are one of Chelsea's biggest rivals and there have been some classic encounters between the two clubs. Have a go at answering these themed questions.

1. In which year did Chelsea first play Tottenham?

2. Who was the first Chelsea manager to lose against Tottenham in the Premier League?

3. Who scored both goals for Chelsea in a 2-1 Premier League win at Wembley in 2017?

4. Chelsea lost 2-1 to Tottenham in the 1967 FA Cup final. Who scored the Blues goal?

5. Who scored a last minute penalty to give Chelsea a win against Tottenham in 1994?

6. Which Blues striker left the club and later joined Tottenham and scored

266 goals for the club?

7. Which Frenchman scored a last minute winner against Spurs in 2006?

8. Which Chelsea youth product scored in his final appearance for the Blues in 1992 before a move to Tottenham?

9. Who scored a perfect hattrick against Tottenham in 2002?

10. Which former Chelsea player led Tottenham to League Cup glory in 1999?

11. In what year did the Blues beat Tottenham 6-1 at White Hart Lane?

12. Who was the first person to manage both Chelsea and Tottenham?

13. Before 2006, when was the last time Tottenham beat Chelsea in any competition?

14. In the 2015/16 season how many yellow cards did Tottenham receive in the game at Stamford Bridge?

15. Who won the Chelsea Player of the Year in 2002 and later played for Tottenham?

16. Which player left Chelsea for Spurs in 1991 with the Blues receiving a record £2.2m for his services?

17. The Blues lost to Tottenham in the League Cup final in 2008. Who scored the Chelsea goal?

18. In 2002, Jimmy Floyd Hasselbaink was sent off against Spurs in a case of mistaken identity. Who should have received the red card?

19. Which African scored on his Chelsea debut against Tottenham?

20. Who was sent off for Spurs in their first game with Chelsea at the Tottenham Hotspur Stadium in 2020?

Answers from quiz What's in a Name?

1 Happy 2 Ball 3 Celestine Babayaro 4 Kevin 5 Leslie 6 Jerrel 7 Mineiro 8 Lynette Osgood 9 Rudi Dil 10 Arsenal 11 Bobby Moore 12 Henry 13 Jorginho 14 Demba Ba 15 Seven 16 Peter Rhoades-Brown 17 Eclipse 18 Mark Hughes 19 Geoff Hurst 20 The Chelsea FC Chronicle

General Knowledge 6

This round tests your Chelsea general knowledge. These are questions that most Blues fans should know but how many will you get correct?

1. Which team did Chelsea beat in the 1955 Charity Shield?

2. How many caps did Peter Bonetti win with England?

3. Against which team did Bobby Tambling score five goals against in a match in 1966?

4. What nationality was Jimmy Windridge?

5. In what year did Kevin De Bruyne make his Chelsea debut?

6. Who were the first Welsh team that the Blues played in a competitive match?

7. Which manager was the Blues boos at the start of the 2011/12 season?

8. How many games did Brian Laudrup play for Chelsea?

9. Which country did Dave Mitchell play for?

10. In which year did the Blues play in a game involving VAR?

11. Who did Chelsea beat in the 2009 FA Cup final?

12. Which company made the Blues kit from 1981 to 1986?

13. Who made his Chelsea debut in the opening game of the 2015/16 season?

14. In which country did the Blues beat Jeunesse Hautcharage 8-0 in 1971?

15. Against which team did Eden Hazard score his 100th Chelsea goal?

16. In what year were the Blues given planning permission to redevelop Stamford Bridge?

17. Which goalkeeper was on the bench for Chelsea in the 2005 League Cup final?

18. Who was given the number 13 shirt in the 2013/14 season?

19. How many goals did Adrian Mutu score for the Blues?

20. Which Merseyside club knocked Chelsea out of the 1991/92 League Cup?

Gianfranco Zola

Gianfranco Zola was once voted the greatest player in the club's history but how much do you know about the little magician?

1. Gianfranco Zola joined Chelsea from which club?

2. How much did the Blues pay for him?

3. Which manager signed him in November 1997?

4. Which team did Zola score his first Chelsea goal against?

5. How many goals did he score for the Blues?

6. How many seasons did Zola play for Chelsea?

7. In what year did the Italian win the FWA Player of the Year award?

8. Who was in goal for Norwich when Gianfranco Zola scored a backheeled flick in a 4-0 win at Stamford Bridge in 2002?

9. Which West Ham defender did Zola give twisted blood to in 1996?

10. In which year did he win the Charity Shield with the Blues?

11. Who passed the ball to Gianfranco Zola before he scored the only goal of the 1998 Cup Winners Cup final?

12. In what year did the Italian score his only Blues hattrick?

13. Zola captained Chelsea for the first time in an FA Cup quarter final in

2000. Who were the opponents?

14. For which club did Gianfranco face Chelsea as a manager at Stamford Bridge in 2008?

15. Which manager announced Zola would be part of his backroom staff in 2018?

16. Gianfranco Zola scored the only goal in a meeting between Italy and England at Wembley in 1997. Which goalkeeper did he score against?

17. Who were the opponents when he scored his last goal for Chelsea?

18. Against which team did the Italian play against in his last game for the Blues?

19. Which club did Zola agree to join after he left Chelsea?

20. Gianfranco Zola appeared in which children's football themed TV show?

Answers from quiz General Knowledge 6

1 Newcastle 2 Seven 3 Aston Villa 4 English 5 2013 6 Cardiff City 7 Andre Villas-Boas 8 Eleven 9 Australia 10 2018 11 Everton 12 Le Coq Sportif 13 Radamel Falcao 14 Luxembourg 15 Watford 16 2017 17 Lenny Pidgley 18 Victor Moses 19 Ten 20 Tranmere Rovers

1960s Chelsea

This set of questions is all about Chelsea in the 1960s decade. How well do you know you club?

1. Who was Chelsea's first manager in the 1960s?
2. Chelsea won the League Cup in 1965. Who did they beat across two legs in the final?
3. In which year did Chelsea win promotion back into Division One?
4. Peter Osgood made his Blues debut in 1964. Who were the opponents?
5. How many hattricks did Jimmy Greaves score in his Chelsea career?
6. The Blues played against Tottenham in the 1967 FA Cup final. Who captained Chelsea on the day?
7. Jimmy Greaves and which other former Blue played for Spurs that day?
8. In what year did the official club colours change to Royal Blue shirt and shorts with white socks?
9. In October 1964 John Hollins became the club's youngest ever captain. Who were the opponents that day?
10. Who was the first player to appear for Chelsea as a substitute?
11. Who was the first player to score as a substitute for the Blues?
12. Who did Chelsea beat in 1966 on the toss of a coin?
13. Which manager resigned in 1967 after the FA gave him a 28 day ban?
14. In what year did Greyhound Racing finish being hosted at Stamford

86

Bridge?

15. In 1969 Bobby Tambling scored his 200th Chelsea goal. Who were the opponents?

16. Which cult hit was first played at Stamford Bridge in 1969 which is still played to this day?

17. From which club did Chelsea sign George Graham from?

18. Which player signed from Aston Villa for a club record of £100,000 in 1966?

19. Who played the most games for the Blues in the decade?

20. In which year did Chelsea first win the FA Youth Cup?

Answers from quiz Gianfranco Zola

1 Parma 2 £4.5m 3 Ruud Gullit 4 Everton 5 80 6 Seven 7 1997 8 Rob Green 9 Julian Dicks 10 2000 11 Dennis Wise 12 1997 13 Gillingham 14 West Ham 15 Maurizio Sarri 16 Ian Walker 17 Everton 18 Liverpool 19 Cagliari 20 Renford Rejects

Almost Impossible 2

This set of questions are as the title suggests. How many of these almost impossible questions can you get correct?

1. What was the name of the Reverend who performed the service during Peter Osgood's funeral?

2. Who was the sculptor of Peter Osgood's statue?

3. What was the name of the ball boy the Eden hazard kicked in 2013?

4. What was the name of the B side on 'Blue is the Colour'?

5. The song 'Liquidator' is performed by Harry J Allstars. What does the 'J' stand for?

6. What was the name of the property development company that bought

Stamford Bridge in the 1980s?

7. Who was the first goalkeeper to make a substitute appearance for Chelsea?

8. Who were the first team to beat Chelsea in a penalty shootout?

9. Which outfield player has made the most appearances for the Blues without scoring a single goal?

10. Which Chelsea player represented Barbados at international level?

11. Which Chelsea player voiced the Green Goblin in French-dubbed version of Spiderman: New Generation?

12. Ron Harris was the player/manager of which club?

13. What was the name of Chelsea's training ground before they moved to Cobham?

14. Which Chelsea player grew up with 17 siblings?

15. Graham Roberts was the head coach of which two international sides?

16. Who did Ruud Gullit appoint as the club's fitness coach in 1996?

17. In 2012, Chelsea partnered with which Formula One racing team?

18. Which Blues star released a song called 'Not the Dancing Kind' in 1984?

19. Which Chelsea player has worked as an underwear model for Calvin Klein?

20. In what year was Chelsea TV launched?

Answers from quiz 1960s Chelsea

1 Ted Drake 2 Leicester City 3 1963 4 Workington Town 5 Thirteen 6 Ron Harris 7 Terry Venables 8 1964 9 Notts County 10 John Boyle 11 Peter Houseman 12 AC Milan 13 Tommy Docherty 14 1968 15 Coventry City 16 Liquidator 17 Aston Villa 18 Tony Hateley 19 Peter Bonetti 20 1960

Backroom Staff

Successful teams rely on more than just the players and manager. Try to answer these questions about the backroom staff from Chelsea's past.

1. Which former player did Frank Lampard announce as one of his assistants in 2019?
2. What nationality was the Blues chairman Bruce Buck?
3. Who became Head of Youth Development in 2011?
4. Who was Roberto Di Matteo's assistant manager when Chelsea won the Champions League in 2012?
5. Which Dr famously quit Chelsea in 2015 after criticism from Jose Mourinho?
6. Who was Ruud Gullit's assistant manager in the 1996/97 season?
7. Michael Emenalo was appointed Chelsea's Technical Director in 2011. which country did he play for?
8. Which chief executive was at the heart of the Blues transfers in the 1990s?
9. In what year did Steve Holland become the club's Assistant Manager?
10. Which manager appointed Ray Wilkins as his assistant in 2008?
11. Who brokered Chelsea's sponsorship deal with Nike in 2016?
12. Which fomer player did Rafa Benitez appoint as his assistant in 2012?
13. Who joined Avram Grant's backroom staff in 2007 after leaving Ajax?
14. Which goalkeeper worked as a trainer and physio for Chelsea in the 1950s, 60s and 70s?
15. What was the name of the Blues goalkeeping coach from 2007 to 2016?
16. What country did the Blues sporting director Frank Arnesen represent?
17. Which reporter, presenter and matchday host left Chelsea in 2016 after 32 years with the club?
18. Who was part of the Blues medical team before becoming David

Beckham's personal manager in 2003?

19. Which masseur once gave a team talk before a Chelsea game against Manchester City in 2014?

20. Who was appointed as Gianluca Vialli's translator in 1998?

Answers from quiz Almost Impossible 2

1 Reverend Martin Swan 2 Philip Jackson 3 Charlie Morgan 4 All Sing Together 5 Johnson 6 Marler Estates 7 Gerry Peyton 8 Luton Town 9 George Smith 10 Michael Gilkes 11 Olivier Giroud 12 Aldershot 13 Harlington 14 Geremi 15 Nepal and Pakistan 16 Ade Mafe 17 Sauber 18 Ruud Gullit 19 Oscar 20 2001

Didier Drogba

Didier Drogba will go down in history as a football legend, especially his time with Chelsea. How many of these questions about the striker can you answer correctly?

1. How many appearances did Didier Drogba make for Chelsea?
2. How many goals did he score for the club?
3. Against which side did he make his debut?
4. Which club did he sign from in 2004?
5. Which country did Didier Drogba play for?
6. How many goals did he score in cup finals?
7. Which team did Drogba score 13 goals against in his Blues career?
8. Didier Drogba was set to take Chelsea's 5th penalty in the 2008 Champions League final. Why didn't he take it?
9. Drogba headed the equalising goal in the 2012 Champions League final from a corner. Who took the corner?
10. He scored the winning penalty in the shootout. Which goalkeeper did

he score against?

11. In which year did he first win the Chelsea Player of the Year?

12. In 2006, Drogba scored a Champions League hattrick. Who were the opponents?

13. When he left the Blues in 2012 he joined Shanghai Shenua in China. Which former Chelsea was already at the club?

14. In 2014, Didier played against Chelsea at Stamford Bridge in the Champions League. Who was he playing for?

15. How many times did he win the Premier League Golden Boot?

16. How many goals did Drogba score in all competitions in the 2009/10 season?

17. In 2012, he became the first African to score 100 Premier League goals. Who were the opponents?

18. Drogba scored the first FA Cup final goal at the new Wembley. Who claimed the assist for the goal?

19. Didier was substituted in his final Chelsea game to a huge reception back in 2015. Who came on to replace him?

20. Which French football team's stadium is called Stade Didier Drogba?

Answers from quiz Backroom Staff

1 Jody Morris 2 American 3 Neil Bath 4 Eddie Newton 5 Eva Carneiro 6 Gwyn Williams 7 Nigeria 8 Colin Hutchinson 9 2009 10 Luiz Felipe Scolari 11 Marina Granovskaia 12 Boudewijn Zenden 13 Henk ten Cate 14 Harry Medhurst 15 Christophe Lollichon 16 Denmark 17 Neil Barnett 18 Terry Byrne 19 Billy McCulloch 20 Gary Staker

Celebrities

Many celebrities have shown an allegiance to Chelsea. How many of these celebrity related questions can you get right?

1. Who was a famous film director and appeared in the film 'Jurassic Park' and directed 'Ghandi'?
2. Which Prime Minister of the 1990s was a Chelsea fan?
3. Who was the lead singer of 'Madness' who also featured on the Blues anthem 'Blue Day'?
4. Who was the lead singer of the band 'Blur'?
5. The song 'Parklife' by Blur featured which English actor?
6. Which Hollywood actor starred in 'Anchorman' and attended the Blues summer tour of America in 2009?
7. In 2013, which popstar announced on Twitter that after 22 years his dad had finally converted him into a Chelsea fan?
8. Which member of the 'Top Gear' TV show was a Blues fan?
9. Which comedian, born in Chelsea, appeared in the films 'Notting Hill' and 'Gladiator' as well as the TV show 'Splash!'?
10. Who hosted 'Soccer AM' in the 1990s and cooking shows such as 'Something for the Weekend'?
11. Which Olympian won a gold medal in the 1,500m in 1980 and 1984?

12. Who won the Men's title at Wimbledon in 1985, 1986 and 1989?

13. What is the name of the actor who played 'Cat' in Red Dwarf?

14. Trevor Nelson was best known for doing what as an occupation?

15. Which Blues fan co-wrote the 1996 England anthem 'It's Coming Home'?

16. Who played Terry McCann in the TV show 'Minder'?

17. Which musician had a hit with '(Everything I Do) I Do It for You' in 1991?

18. What was the name of the TV chef who wrote 'How to be a Domestic Goddess'?

19. Which former England footballer was famous for doing his 'Robot' goal celebration?

20. Who is famous for saying 'You're only supposed to blow the bloody doors off!' in the film 'The Italian Job'?

Answers from quiz Didier Drogba

1 381 2 164 3 Manchester Utd 4 Marseille 5 Ivory Coast 6 Nine 7 Arsenal 8 He had been sent off in extra time. 9 Juan Mata 10 Manuel Neuer 11 2010 12 Levski Sofia 13 Nicolas Anelka 14 Galatasaray 15 Two 16 37 17 Stoke City 18 Frank Lampard 19 Diego Costa 20 Levallois SC

General Knowledge 7

This round tests your Chelsea general knowledge. These are questions that most Blues fans should know but how many will you get correct?

1. In what year did David Lee make his debut for the Blues?

2. Who were the first German team to play Chelsea in a competitive match?

3. How many FA Cup finals did Salomon Kalou play in with the Blues?

4. Who scored in his final Chelsea appearance against Sheffield Utd in 1992?

5. Against which club did Paul Canoville receive his only red card with the Blues?

6. In which year did Chelsea first play a competitive match in Portugal?

7. Who did the Blues play in the 2007 League Cup semi-final?

8. What nickname was given to Chelsea under Ted Drake's management?

9. Which country did Mikael Forssell play for?

10. How many red cards did Frank Leboeuf receive during his Chelsea career?

11. Which player scored two own goals with the Blues in the 2006/07 season?

12. In what year did Eddie McCreadie take charge of Chelsea?

13. Who was sent off twice for the Blues in the 2017/18 season?

14. How many players did Chelsea use in the 2004/05 season?

15. Who was the first Northern Irish manager of the Blues?

16. In which county is Chelsea's training ground in Cobham set?

17. Who were the Blues shirt sponsors for the 2000 FA Cup final?

18. Which player scored twice in the 2005 Champions League final while on loan from Chelsea?

19. How league many points did the Blues win in the 1988/89 season?

20. Which brothers played for Chelsea in the 1967 FA Cup final?

Answers from quiz Celebrities

1 Richard Attenborough 2 John Major 3 Suggs 4 Damon Albarn 5 Phil Daniels 6 Will Ferrell 7 Ed Sheeran 8 Jeremy Clarkson 9 Omid Djalili 10 Tim Lovejoy 11 Seb Coe 12 Boris Becker 13 Danny John-Jules 14 DJ 15 David Baddiel 16 Dennis Waterman 17 Bryan Adams 18 Nigella Lawson 19 Peter Crouch 20 Michael Caine

Spain

The Spanish influence on Chelsea cannot be forgotten. How many of these themed related questions can you get right?

1. Who was the first Spaniard to play for Chelsea?
2. Which player signed from Liverpool for £50m in 2011?
3. Who won the Chelsea Player of the Year in 2012 and 2013?
4. Which Spaniard was captain for the 2019 Europa League final?
5. In what year did Chelsea sign Cesc Fabregas?
6. Who scored against the Blues in the 2014 Champions League semi-final before joining the club that summer?
7. Pedro scored on his Chelsea debut in 2015. Who were the opponents?
8. Which Spaniard played against the Blues with Sunderland in 2014 before joining Chelsea two years later?
9. Kepa Arrizabalaga scored an own goal with Chelsea in 2019. Who were the opponents?
10. Which Spaniard was sent off against Norwich as a substitute in an FA Cup match in 2018?
11. Enrique De Lucas signed for Chelsea in 2002. Which club did he come from?
12. In which year did Asier Del Horno make his debut for the Blues?
13. Which Spaniard was an unused substitute for Chelsea in the 2012 Champions League final?
14. Who knocked the Blues out of the 1994/95 UEFA Cup Winners Cup?
15. Who scored for Chelsea against Barcelona at Stamford Bridge in the 2011/12 season?
16. In which year did the Blues first face a Spanish side in a competitive match?

17. Who was sent off for Liverpool against Chelsea in February 2006?

18. Which Spaniard scored against the Blues in the 2005 League Cup final?

19. Which team did Rafa Benitez manage after leaving Chelsea in 2013?

20. Who were the first team the Blues beat in Spain?

Answers from quiz General Knowledge 7

1 1988 2 TSV Munich 3 Three 4 Jason Cundy 5 Brighton & Hove Albion 6 2004 7 Wycombe Wanderers 8 Drake's Ducklings 9 Finland 10 Five 11 Michael Essien 12 1975 13 Pedro 14 Thirty 15 Danny Blanchflower 16 Surrey 17 Autoglass 18 Hernan Crespo 19 99 20 Ron and Allan Harris

Missing Letters 1

Fill in the missing letters to reveal the name of someone from Chelsea's history.

1. _I_I_R _R_G_A (6,6)

2. _D_N _A_A_D (4,6)

3. _O_N _E_R (4,5)

4. _E_R _E_H (4,4)

5. _I_N_R_N_O _O_A (10,4)

6. _E_N_S _I_E (6,4)

7. _A_Y _A_I_L (4,6)

8. _E_C _A_R_G_S (4,8)

9. _S_L_Y _O_E (6,4)

10. _A_C_L E_A_L_Y (6,8)

11. _L_N _U_S_N (4,6)

12. _O_Y _O_R_S (4,6)

13. _A_I_E_ (7)

14. _A_E _E_S_N_ (4,7)

15. _O_N _P_N_E_ (4,7)

16. _U_N _A_A (4,4)

17. _I_T_R _O_E_ (6,5)

18. _A_I_N _U_F (6,4)

19. _A_K _U_H_S (4,6)

20. _U_T _O_M_ (4,5)

Top Goalscorers

Everyone loves a goalscorer. Just name the Chelsea player who scored the most goals for the Blues in the seasons shown in this set of questions.

1. 2011/12

2. 1905/06

3. 2018/19

4. 1996/97

5. 1969/70

6. 1954/55

7. 2003/04

8. 1983/84

9. 1999/00

10. 2014/15

11. 1995/96

12. 1975/76

13. 2009/10

14. 1987/88

15. 1960/61

16. 2012/13

17. 1997/98

18. 1981/82

19. 1970/71

20. 1964/65

Answers from quiz Missing Letters 1

1 Didier Drogba 2 Eden Hazard 3 John Terry 4 Petr Cech 5 Gianfranco Zola 6 Dennis Wise 7 Gary Cahill 8 Cesc Fabregas 9 Ashley Cole 10 Marcel Desailly 11 Alan Hudson 12 Jody Morris 13 Ramires 14 Dave Beasant 15 John Spencer 16 Juan Mata 17 Victor Moses 18 Damien Duff 19 Mark Hughes 20 Kurt Zouma

True or False 6

Read the following questions. Just simply answer True or False for each question.

1. Chelsea went unbeaten in 86 consecutive home games between 2004 and 2008.

2. The Blues lost 8-1 away at Wolverhampton Wanderers in 1953.

3. In the 1976/77 season Chelsea failed to keep any clean sheets during the league campaign.

4. Frank Lampard was once the club's record signing.

5. Chelsea only conceded 15 league goals in the 2004/05 season.

6. Dennis Wise was booked more times than he scored for the Blues.

7. Salomon Kalou never signed autographs before a match as he believed it was bad luck.

8. Chelsea drew more games than they won during the 1994/95 season.

9. Claude Makelele grew up in Ghana.

10. Stamford the Lion was stolen in 2005.

11. Stamford Bridge used to hold midget car racing.

12. In 1987 Tony Cascarino was arrested for tax evasion.

13. The Blues played in the third tier of English football between 1928 and 1930.

14. The film The Football Factory is based on Chelsea hooliganism.

15. Antonio Conte was the first Italian to win the Premier League as a manager.

16. In 2012 Chelsea became the only team in London with a European Cup.

17. Willian scored a brace against Chelsea before joining the Blues the following season.

18. Ron Harris never scored an own goal in his entire career.

19. Four members of the 1988 FA Cup winning Wimbledon later went on to play for Chelsea.

20. Mark Schwarzer was born in Germany.

Answers from quiz Top Goalscorers

1 Frank Lampard 2 Frank Pearson 3 Eden Hazard 4 Mark Hughes 5 Peter Osgood 6 Roy Bentley 7 Jimmy Floyd Hasselbaink 8 Kerry Dixon 9 Tore Andre Flo 10 Diego Costa 11 John Spencer 12 Ray Wilkins 13 Didier Drogba 14 Gordon Durie 15 Jimmy Greaves 16 Fernando Torres 17 Gianluca Vialli 18 Clive Walker 19 Keith Weller 20 Barry Bridges

Anagrams 2

The classic game of anagrams. Rearrange the letters to reveal the names of these Chelsea related puzzles.

1. DOORSTEP EGO

2. EVER TACKLES

3. DEAD EVIL

4. RADICALS VOTED

5. CRAYON ACTIONS

6. FERRET BARREL

7. CAMEL SPANKING

8. DENTAL ROOFER

9. SPANNER CHORE

10. THIN BLUE KID

11. INK MASTER

12. CODE

13. MAD BABE

14. OSTRICH NUTS

15. RECTAL COLON

16. HORSE MOMENTO

17. SHAMROCK BIN

18. SNAKE BET

19. RANK GERM SNOT

20. TINKLE HOLES

Managers

Many fans debate who clubs should sign, play and the tactics the team play. How many of these Chelsea manager related questions can you get correct?

1. Who was the Chelsea manager when they won the Champions League in 2012?

2. Which country was Antonio Conte the manager of before he joined the Blues?

3. Maurizio Sarri left Chelsea to join which club?

4. Who was the Blues manager in the 2012 FIFA World Club cup?

5. Which manager signed Ruud Gullit as a player for Chelsea?

6. What drink did Gianluca Vialli give to his players before his first game as Chelsea manager?

7. What nationality was Luiz Felipe Scolari?

8. Ruud Gullit left the Blues in 1998. Which other Premier League team did he manage?

9. Who was the Chelsea manager when they won the FA Cup in 2009?

10. Carlo Ancelotti was sacked as the Blues boss after finishing in which league position?

11. Which former Portuguese manager served as an assistant under Jose Mourinho at the club?

12. What nationality was Avram Grant?

13. Who was the Blues boss for their first game in the Premier League?

14. Who became the first ever person to win the football league as a manager and a player?

15. Which manager was also known as 'The Tinkerman'?

16. Who became Chelsea manager after David Calderhead left the club in 1933?

17. Who was the Blues boss during WW2?

18. Which manager resigned after being refused a company car in 1977?

19. How many games did Bobby Gould oversee as the Blues boss?

20. In which year did John Hollins become Chelsea manager?

Answers from quiz Anagrams 2

1 Peter Osgood 2 Steve Clarke 3 David Lee 4 David Rocastle 5 Tony Cascarino 6 Albert Ferrer 7 Nigel Spackman 8 Tore Andre Flo 9 Hernan Crespo 10 Keith Dublin 11 Mark Stein 12 Deco 13 Demba Ba 14 Chris Sutton 15 Carlton Cole 16 Emerson Thome 17 Mark Bosnich 18 Ken Bates 19 Ken Armstrong 20 Ken Shellito

Frank Lampard

Super Frankie Lampard was one of the club's most loved and greatest ever players. How much do you know about him?

1. Which club sold Frank Lampard to Chelsea back in 2001?

2. How much did the Blues buy Frank Lampard for?

3. Which position did Frank Lampard play in?

4. What squad number did he wear during his time with Chelsea?

5. Frank Lampard made his Chelsea debut against which side?

6. Against which team did Lampard score his first Chelsea goal?

7. What was unusual about Frank Lampard's penalty vs West Ham in 2009?

8. How many penalties did Lampard score for Chelsea (excluding

shootouts)?

9. Lampard was named as captain for the first time in 2003. Who were Chelsea's opponents?

10. Which American club did Frank Lampard play for?

11. Frank scored in a Champions League final for Chelsea. Who were the opponents?

12. Lampard scored against Chelsea in the Premier League the season after leaving the Blues. Who was he playing for?

13. How is Harry Redknapp related to Frank Lampard?

14. What is the name of Lampard's autobiography?

15. Who did Frank marry in 2015?

16. Who were the opponents when Lampard scored his 200th Chelsea goal?

17. Who were Chelsea's opponents when he became the club's all-time leading goalscorer?

18. Frank Lampard appeared as a team captain in what comedy panel show?

19. How many international caps did he win as a Chelsea player?

20. In 2005, Lampard came second in the Ballon D'Or. Which player came first?

Answers from quiz Managers

1 Roberto Di Matteo 2 Italy 3 Juventus 4 Rafa Benitez 5 Glenn Hoddle 6 Champagne 7 Brazilian 8 Newcastle Utd 9 Guus Hiddink 10 2nd 11 Andre Villas-Boas 12 Israeli 13 Ian Porterfield 14 Ted Drake 15 Claudio Ranieri 16 Leslie Knighton 17 Billy Birrell 18 Eddie McCreadie 19 Two 20 1985

Chelsea Women

In 1921 Women's football was banned for fifty years. Ever since it returned it has become an ever increasing game with Chelsea contributing towards it. How much do you know about the women's team?

1. What were Chelsea FC Women known as before a name change in 2018?

2. In which year were the team formed?

3. Who became their manager in 2012?

4. Eni Aluko left Chelsea to join which Italian club?

5. Who was the PFA Women's Players' Player of the Year in 2018?

6. In what year did they first win the FA Women's Super League?

7. What competition did they win in the 2019/20 season?

8. Who was sent off for England against the United States in the 2019 World Cup semi-final?

9. How many FA Women's FA Cup final wins did Katie Chapman have in her career?

10. Who did Chelsea beat in the 2017/18 FA Women's Cup final?

11. In which year did Gilly Flaherty make her Blues debut?

12. Who was named as the club captain in September 2019?

13. Which country did Claire Rafferty represent at international level?

14. Who scored the only goal of the game when the Blues won the first Women's FA Cup final to be held at Wembley?

15. In which year did Stamford Bridge host its first women's football match?

16. What country did Erin Cuthbert represent at the 2019 FIFA Women's World Cup?

17. Who scored twice for Chelsea in the 2017/18 FA Women's Cup final?

18. How many times did the Blues win the Surrey County Cup between 2003 and 2013?

19. Who did Chelsea lose to in the 2012 FA Women's Cup final?

20. The Blues signed Sophie Ingle from which club in 2018?

Answers from quiz Frank Lampard

1 West Ham 2 £11m 3 Midfield 4 8 5 Newcastle Utd 6 Levski Sofia 7 He had to take it three times. 8 49 9 Arsenal 10 New York City FC 11 Manchester United 12 Manchester City 13 Uncle 14 Totally Frank 15 Christine Bleakley 16 West Ham 17 Aston Villa 18 Play to the Whistle 19 104 20 Ronaldinho

1950s Chelsea

This set of questions is all about Chelsea in the 1950s decade. How well do you know you club?

1. Who was Chelsea's first manager in the 1950s?

2. Chelsea won the League title in 1955. Who was the club captain?

3. What was the name of Chelsea's manager that led them to the title?

4. Which team finished runners up to the Blues in 1955?

5. In 1951 Chelsea survived relegation by goal average. What was goal average difference?

6. Chelsea used floodlights at Stamford Bridge for the first time in 1957. Who were the opponents?

7. Which two players scored a joint own goal in Chelsea's favour back in 1954?

8. Chelsea were the 1st English side to travel by aeroplane back from a domestic away match. Which team did they play?

9. The Blues played their first ever European game in 1958. Who were the opponents?

10. Roy Bentley was the first player to score 150 goals for Chelsea. Who did he score his last goal against?

11. In what year did Chelsea first appear in the FA Youth Cup final?

12. In 1959 two players scored on their Blues debut in a 3-2 win against West Ham. Bobby Tambling was one but who was the other?

13. Which Chelsea player represented England in the 1950 World Cup?

14. England's 1966 World Cup winning manager Ron Greenwood made his Blues debut in which year?

15. In August 1958 Jimmy Greaves scored 5 goals in one match for Chelsea. Who were the opponents?

16. In which year did Chelsea last play on Christmas Day?

17. Chelsea beat Portsmouth on Christmas Day 1957. What was the score?

18. From which club did Chelsea sign Peter Sillett from?

19. Who played the most games for the Blues in the decade?

20. Which country was Frank Mitchell born in?

Answers from quiz Chelsea Women

1 Chelsea Ladies 2 1992 3 Emma Hayes 4 Juventus 5 Fran Kirby 6 2015 7 FA Women's League Cup 8 Millie Bright 9 Ten 10 Arsenal 11 2014 12 Magdalena Eriksson 13 England 14 Ji So-Yun 15 1920 16 Scotland 17 Ramona Bachmann 18 Nine 19 Birmingham City 20 Liverpool

Scotland

England's auld enemy actually had a big impact on the club, especially in its formative years. Test your Scotland related knowledge.

1. Who was Chelsea's first Scottish manager?

2. Which Scotsman played for the Blues in the 1997 FA Cup final?

3. Who won the Chelsea Player of the Year in 1987?

4. Which Scotsman became the Blues record signing in 1992?

5. In what year did John Spencer run 80 yards to score a solo goal for Chelsea in the UEFA Cup Winners Cup?

6. Which Scotsman was the first to wear the number 26 shirt for the Blues?

7. How many of Chelsea's 1915 FA Cup final side were Scottish?

8. Who scored an own goal in the 1986 Full Members Cup final?

9. Which player scored twice on his Chelsea debut in 1982?

10. In which year did Charlie Cooke play his last game for the Blues?

11. Which Scotsman made his Chelsea debut in 2005?

12. George Graham left the Blues in 1966. Which team did he join?

13. Which manager gave Joe McLaughlin his Chelsea debut?

14. Who were the Blues opponents from Scotland in the 1968/69 Fairs Cup?

15. Which Scotsman took charge of over 900 Chelsea games in the 1900s?

16. Who was the Blues manager when the club won the League Cup in 1965?

17. Which Scotsman played in both the 1986 and 1990 Full Members Cup finals?

18. In which year did Ian Porterfield become Chelsea's manager?

19. Which Scotsman scored a hattrick as a substitute against Chelsea for Everton in 2015?

20. Ray Wilkins was given the Blues captaincy by which manager?

Answers from quiz 1950s Chelsea

1 Billy Birrell 2 Roy Bentley 3 Ted Drake 4 Wolverhampton Wanderers 5 0.044 of a goal 6 Sparta Prague 7 Stanley Milburn and Jack Froggatt 8 Newcastle Utd 9 Frem Copenhagen 10 Blackpool 11 1958 12 Barry Bridges 13 Roy Bentley 14 1952 15 Wolverhampton Wanderers 16 1958 17 7-4 18 Southampton 19 Ken Armstrong 20 Australia

Previous Club 3

Look at the players in this set of questions. From which club did Chelsea sign them from?

1. Kerry Dixon

2. Steve Clarke

3. Pat Nevin

4. Paul Canoville

5. Micky Droy

6. John Hollins

7. Ian Hutchinson

8. David Webb

9. Eddie McCreadie

10. Roy Bentley

11. Willie Foulke

12. Salomon Kalou

13. Carlo Cudicini

14. Slavisa Jokanovic

15. Kevin Hitchcock

16. David Speedie

17. Tore Andre Flo

18. Tony Cascarino

19. Eddie Niedzwiecki

20. Petar Borota

Answers from quiz Scotland

1 John Tait Robertson 2 Steve Clarke 3 Pat Nevin 4 Robert Fleck 5 1994 6 Andy Dow 7 Four 8 Doug Rougvie 9 David Speedie 10 1978 11 Steven Watt 12 Arsenal 13 John Neal 14 Greenock Morton 15 David Calderhead 16 Tommy Docherty 17 Kevin McAllister 18 1991 19 Steven Naismith 20 Eddie McCreadie

London Rivals

London is full of football clubs which allows for many different rivalries in the capital. How many of these questions related to other London clubs can you get right?

1. Which of Chelsea's football league rivals are situated closest to Stamford Bridge?

2. Which West London side did the Blues beat in the 1970 FA Cup quarter finals?

3. In April 2012 Chelsea beat QPR 6-1. Which player scored a hattrick?

4. Which London club did the Blues play in 1950 and then not again until 2013?

5. Chelsea signed Joe Cole for £6m from which club in 2003?

6. In April 2006 the Blues beat West Ham 4-1 despite being reduced to ten men in the first half. Which Chelsea player was sent off?

7. Which club did Vinnie Jones join after leaving the Blues in 1992?

8. Who did Chelsea sign from Wimbledon in 1980 and then sold back to them in 1983?

9. In which year did the Blues play their last game against Wimbledon at Plough Lane?

10. Who did Chelsea play in their first London derby in the football league?

11. The Blues won the Football League (South) Cup Final in 1945. Who were the opponents?

12. Chelsea lost to Millwall in a penalty shootout is 1995. Who missed the Blues final spot kick?

13. John Spencer left Chelsea to join which other London club?

14. Who won the Champions League with the Blues in 2012 before signing for QPR that summer?

15. Which London team did the Blues play in the 3rd round of the FA Cup in the 1993/94 season?

16. What was the name of the Chelsea manager's brother who played for Barnet that season?

17. Which Chelsea player was sent off against Arsenal in the 2017 Community Shield?

18. Who was sent off for Tottenham by VAR after appearing to kick Antonio Rudiger in 2019?

19. In 1966, Ron Harris scored for Chelsea and then netted an own goal a minute later against which London side?

20. Jimmy Greaves scored on his Blues debut. Who were the opponents?

1 Reading 2 St Mirren 3 Clyde 4 Hillingdon Borough 5 Slough Town 6 Arsenal 7 Cambridge Utd 8 Southampton 9 East Stirling 10 Newcastle 11 Sheffield United 12 Feyenoord 13 Castel Di Sangro 14 Deportivo La Coruna 15 Mansfield Town 16 Darlington 17 Brann Bergen 18 Celtic 19 Wrexham 20 Partizan Belgrade

General Knowledge 8

This round tests your Chelsea general knowledge. These are questions that most Blues fans should know but how many will you get correct?

1. Which Liverpool player scored an own goal in the 2005 League Cup final?

2. What country did Kevin Wilson play for between 1987 and 1995?

3. How many goals did Geremi score for Chelsea?

4. Which former Chelsea player was Fulham manager against the Blues in 2019?

5. Who was the first player to score a hattrick against Chelsea in the Premier League?

6. In which year did Jose Mourinho first take charge of a team against the Blues?

7. Which manager was in charge of Real Madrid against Chelsea in the 1998 UEFA Super Cup?

8. How many Premier League titles did Petr Cech win with the Blues?

9. Who was the first player to be sent off against Chelsea for two different clubs?

10. What country did Jakob Kjeldbjerg represent?

11. Which former Chelsea midfielder was in charge of Sunderland when they knocked the Blues out of the 2013/14 League Cup?

12. In what year did Roy Bentley make his Chelsea debut?

13. Which player scored two penalties for the Blues in a game against Ajax in 2019?

14. Who did Chelsea beat in the 2012 Champions League quarter final?

15. What was the score when the Blues beat Everton in the 2008/09 FA Cup final?

16. Chelsea played Rosenborg in the 2007/08 Champions League. Which country are they from?

17. Gary Pallister scored own goals against the Blues with Man Utd and which other club?

18. How much did Chelsea pay West Ham to sign Joe Cole in 2003?

19. Who wore the number 2 shirt for the Blues before Branislav Ivanovic?

20. In which year did Eidur Gudjohnsen score his only hattrick for Chelsea?

Answers from quiz London Rivals

1 Fulham 2 QPR 3 Fernando Torres 4 Brentford 5 West Ham 6 Maniche 7 Wimbledon 8 Phil Driver 9 1989 10 Clapton Orient 11 Millwall 12 John Spencer 13 QPR 14 Jose Bosingwa 15 Barnet 16 Carl Hoddle 17 Pedro 18 Son Heung-Min 19 West Ham 20 Tottenham

Strikers

There have been so many great strikers in Chelsea's history. Some have been less successful. Try to answer these questions about these forwards.

1. Which Chelsea legend scored 164 goals in 381 appearances for the club?

2. What shirt number did Gianfranco Zola wear in his time with the Blues?

3. Who scored 193 goals for Chelsea between 1983 and 1992?

4. Which striker signed for a club record of £30m in 2006?

5. Diego Costa scored for the Blues on his debut. Who were the opponents?

6. Which striker missed a penalty in the 2008 Champions League final penalty shootout?

7. Hernan Crespo represented which country at international level?

8. In which year did Gianluca Vialli sign for the Blues?

9. Which club did Chelsea sign Chris Sutton from in a club record £10m move in 1999?

10. Who scored in every round of the 1969/70 FA Cup run?

11. Which striker scored five goals on his Chelsea debut?

12. How many goals did Radamel Falcao score in his Blues career?

13. Which club did Roy Bentley join after leaving Chelsea?

14. How many goals did Jimmy Greaves score in his Blues career?

15. Who did Chelsea sign from Darlington in 1982 and went on to score a hattrick for Chelsea in a cup final?

16. What country did Tore Andre Flo represent at international level?

17. Who signed for Chelsea from Newcastle for £25,000 in 1930?

18. Pierluigi Casiraghi played his last ever game of football with Chelsea before retiring through injury. Who were the opponents?

19. Which striker scored against his former club in the 2019 Europa League final?

20. Who won Chelsea's Player of the Year award in 1997?

Answers from quiz General Knowledge 8

1 Steven Gerrard 2 Northern Ireland 3 Four 4 Scott Parker 5 Dion Dublin 6 2010 7 Guus Hiddink 8 Four 9 Tal Ben-Haim 10 Denmark 11 Gus Poyet 12 1948 13 Jorginho 14 Benfica 15 2-1 16 Norway 17 Middlesbrough 18 £6m 19 Glen Johnson 20 2004

Awards

Success in football is often measured by trophies and awards. How many of these theme related questions can you get correct?

1. Who won the first ever Chelsea Player of the Year in 1967?

2. The Chelsea Players' Player of the Year started in 2006. Who was the first winner?

3. The Young Player of the Year award began in 1983. Who was the first recipient?

4. The Mayor of which city declared the 1st of September 2016 as Frank Lampard Day?

5. Which Chelsea player was awarded a CBE by the Queen in 2012 for services to Equality and Diversity in Football?

6. In which year was Gianfranco Zola awarded an honorary OBE?

7. Which player won the FWA Player of the Year award in 2017?

8. Who was the first overseas player to win the Chelsea Player of the Year award?

9. Which player won the Young Player of the Year in three consecutive from 2003 to 2005?

10. Who was named FIFA's best Men's goalkeeper in 2018?

11. Which former Chelsea player won the Ferenc Puskas award for the best goal in 2012?

12. Frank Leboeuf played a doctor in which Oscar winning film?

13. Which player won a Gold medal at the 1912 Olympics for football while under contract at Chelsea?

14. Peter Bonetti and Peter Osgood top the UK Music charts with the 1970 World Cup squad. What was the name of the song?

15. Which Chelsea player won a gold medal with Spain in the 1992 Olympic

games?

16. Who won a gold medal with Nigeria in the 1996 Olympics before joining the Blues a year later?

17. Who did Ruud Gullit dedicate his 1987 World Player of the Year award to?

18. Which Englishman won the Chelsea Goal of the Season award for the 2009/10 season?

19. Who was the first person to win the Chelsea Player of the Year award on three occasions?

20. Which player was awarded both the Military Medal and Distinguished Conduct Medal for gallantry and died in 1917?

Answers from quiz Strikers

1 Didier Drogba 2 25 3 Kerry Dixon 4 Andriy Shevchenko 5 Burnley 6 Nicolas Anelka 7 Argentina 8 1996 9 Blackburn Rovers 10 Peter Osgood 11 George Hilsdon 12 One 13 Fulham 14 132 15 David Speedie 16 Norway 17 Hughie Gallacher 18 West Ham 19 Olivier Giroud 20 Mark Hughes

True or False 7

Read the following questions. Just simply answer True or False for each question.

1. In a game vs Southern Utd in 1905 the Blues played without a recognised goalkeeper.

2. Ron Suart played for Chelsea in the 1950s.

3. Chris Sutton scored all three of his goals for the Blues with his head.

4. Denis Law scored in seven consecutive appearances against Chelsea between 1960 and 1965.

5. Jose Mourinho is the only person to be the Blues boss on more than one

occasion.

6. Vivian Woodward missed the 1915 FA Cup final as a tree had fallen through his roof.

7. Juan Mata, Fernando Torres and Oscar all played 64 games each for Chelsea in the 2012/13 season.

8. Micky Hazard became a taxi driver after he retired from football.

9. Gianfranco Zola appeared in the music video for Bonnie Tyler's 'Total Eclipse of the Heart'.

10. Teddy Maybank appeared on the TV show Blind Date.

11. Jim Molyneux was the first Chelsea player with the letter 'x' in his surname.

12. Doug Rougvie scored more own goals for the opposition than he did for the Blues.

13. Michael Duberry owned a nightclub in North London called Doobs.

14. Scott Sinclair signed for the Blues from Bristol City.

15. Ruud Gullit was the first overseas manager to win the FA Cup.

16. Michael Ballack was the first German to score for Chelsea.

17. Steve Kember became the Blues record signing in 1971.

18. Maurizio Sarri used to smoke cigarettes on the touchline during his managerial career in Italy.

19. Blue is the Colour was written by Rod Stewart.

20. Chris Sutton was declared bankrupt in 2014.

Who Are Ya? 2

Read the clues to work out which person from the Blues history it is talking about.

1. Signed from Stratsbourg for £2.5m before winning the World Cup in 1998.

2. Died in 2018 after scoring 150 goals for the Blues.

3. A Chelsea TV presenter who made his Chelsea debut in 1974 aged just sixteen years old.

4. Became Chelsea manager in the 1990s after leaving Swindon Town.

5. Made his debut in 1978 and made over 400 appearances for Chelsea.

6. A defender who won the league in 1955 playing alongside his brother John.

7. Won the Champions League with Porto in 2004 before scoring two goals in 217 games for Chelsea.

8. A striker who signed for the Blues in 2013 and admitted to be addicted to strawberry syrup.

9. A right back won the Chelsea Player of the Year in 1974.

10. Signed from Benfica in 2010 before moving to China in 2016.

11. A Chelsea youth product who became England's assistant manager under Roy Hodgson in 2012.

12. Signed from Atletico Madrid in 2014 and scored seven goals in his first four league games.

13. Danish midfielder who was part of a swap deal with Brian Laudrup in 1998.

14. Olympic gold medallist in 2000 who scored against Chelsea with Barcelona, Inter Milan and Everton.

15. Won the Premier League in 2005 and 2006 before playing for Tottenham and Arsenal.

16. Spanish midfielder who was said to have had a magic hat.

17. Signed from Ipswich in 1987 and mainly recognised for a moustache.

18. Won the Premier League in 2016 and 2017 with different clubs.

19. Married a member of the girl group 'The Saturdays' and appeared in I'm a Celeb... in 2016.

20. Midfielder and manager whose son won Strictly Come Dancing in 2009.

Answers from quiz True or False 7

1 True 2 False 3 False 4 True 5 False 6 False 7 True 8 True 9 False 10 True 11 True 12 False 13 False 14 False 15 True 16 False 17 True 18 True 19 False 20 True

Testimonials

After ten years with a club players were often rewarded with a testimonial match. Have a go at answering these testimonial themed questions.

1. In what year did Chelsea first participate in a testimonial match?

2. The first ever testimonial at Stamford Bridge was for two players. Who were they?

3. Who were Chelsea's opponents in Eddie Niedzwiecki's testimonial back in 1989?

4. Which goalkeeper scored two penalties in Bobby Tambling's testimonial?

5. Which player missed a penalty in his own testimonial vs Man Utd back in 1974?

6. Which Manchester United legend played for a Chelsea Past XI in Peter Osgood's testimonial?

7. Which famous cricketer played in Ron Harris' testimonial in 1980?

8. Which Spanish team did Chelsea play in John Bumstead's testimonial?

9. Chelsea drew 0-0 vs Bologna in 1999. Whose testimonial was this for?

10. Who were the opponents in Ron Harris' first testimonial?

11. Who came on as a substitute to replace Kerry Dixon in Dixon's benefit match vs Tottenham in 1995?

12. Who was the Porto manager when they played Chelsea in Paul Elliott's benefit match?

13. Chelsea lost to PSV Eindhoven in Steve Clarke's benefit match. Which player scored the winning goal and signed for the Blues five years later?

14. Who was the first Chelsea player to score in his own testimonial?

15. Chelsea beat a London XI in John Mortimore's testimonial in 1966. What was the score?

16. The Blues played an International XI in an Ian Hutchinson's testimonial. How many of that team played for Chelsea at some point?

17. How many goals did Ian Hutchinson score in his own testimonial game vs QPR in 1978?

18. Who were Chelsea's opponents in Charlie Cooke's testimonial?

19. The Blues played an International XI in John Dempsey's testimonial in 1980. Which Portuguese Ballon D'Or winner played for them?

20. Which father and son duo have both had testimonials involving Chelsea?

Answers from quiz Who Are Ya? 2

1 Frank Leboeuf 2 Roy Bentley 3 Tommy Langley 4 Glenn Hoddle 5 John

Bumstead 6 Peter Sillett 7 Paulo Ferreira 8 Demba Ba 9 Gary Locke 10 Ramires 11 Ray Lewington 12 Diego Costa 13 Bjarne Goldbaek 14 Samuel Eto'o 15 William Gallas 16 Cesc Fabregas 17 Kevin Wilson 18 N'Golo Kante 19 Wayne Bridge 20 John Hollins

Next Club 3

Look at the players in this set of questions. Name the club they joined after leaving Chelsea.

1. Bjarne Goldbaek

2. Marcel Desailly

3. Eddie Newton

4. Mark Hughes

5. Erland Johnsen

6. John Spencer

7. Kerry Dixon

8. Kevin Wilson

9. John Bumstead

10. Paul Canoville

11. Joey Jones

12. Mickey Thomas

13. Clive Walker

14. Ron Harris

15. Tommy Baldwin

16. Bobby Tambling

17. Jimmy Greaves

18. Willie Foulke

19. George Hilsdon

20. Deco

Answers from quiz Testimonials

1 1905 (vs Southampton) 2 Harold Miller and George Mills 3 Chelsea 1983/84 team 4 Peter Bonetti 5 Eddie McCreadie 6 George Best 7 Ian Botham 8 Real Sociedad 9 Dennis Wise 10 Glasgow Rangers 11 Dave Beasant 12 Bobby Robson 13 Boudewijn Zenden 14 Micky Droy 15 Chelsea won 9-7 16 Nine 17 Two 18 Crystal Palace 19 Eusebio 20 Keith and Gavin Peacock

Milestones

Milestones in football are often talked about and form an important part of history. How well do you know about the milestones in the club's history?

1. Who did Chelsea play in their 100th competitive match?

2. Which team did the Blues score their 100th goal against?

3. Who was the first Chelsea player to make 100 appearances for the club?

4. In what year did the Blues have their 100th player sent off?

5. Who did Chelsea play in their 200th competitive match?

6. Which team did the Blues score their 200th goal against?

7. Who was the first Chelsea player to make 200 appearances for the club?

8. Who was the first player to score 200 goals for Chelsea?

9. Who did Chelsea play in their 500th competitive match?

10. Which team did the Blues score their 500th goal against?

11. Who was the first Chelsea player to make 500 appearances for the club?

12. Who was the 500th person to play for the Blues?

13. In what year did the Blues play their 1,000th game?

14. Who was the first player to win 1,000 league points with Chelsea?

15. Which player became the first to cost the Blues over £1,000?

16. In 2017 Chelsea played their 5,000th competitive match. Who were the

opponents?

17. Who scored Chelsea's 5,000th goal in 1985?

18. Who were the opponents the first time Chelsea played in front of a crowd of 10,000 back in 1905?

19. In what year did the Blues first field a teenager in the starting line-up?

20. In what year did Chelsea first field a player aged over 40 years old?

Answers from quiz Next Club 3

1 Fulham 2 Al Gharafa 3 Birmingham 4 Southampton 5 Rosenborg 6 QPR 7 Southampton 8 Notts County 9 Charlton Athletic 10 Reading 11 Huddersfield Town 12 West Brom 13 Sunderland 14 Brentford 15 Gravesend 16 Crystal Palace 17 AC Milan 18 Bradford City 19 West Ham 20 Fluminense

General Knowledge 9

This round tests your Chelsea general knowledge. These are questions that most Blues fans should know but how many will you get correct?

1. What colour socks did Chelsea wear in the 1970 FA Cup final replay?

2. Who was the Blues unused goalkeeper in the 2012 Champions League final?

3. How many times did Chelsea play Burnley in the 1955/56 season?

4. Who was told his dad had been kidnapped just hours before he played in a World Cup match in 2018?

5. Which country did Mario Stanic represent at international level?

6. What position did Ben Sahar play?

7. Who was the first club Mark Hughes managed against Chelsea back in 2004?

8. In which decade did Eric Parsons play for the Blues?

9. Who came 6th in the 1970 London to Mexico World Cup Rally car race?

10. What country did Joey Jones play for?

11. In what season did Ruben-Loftus Cheek make his Chelsea debut?

12. Who scored the Blues Goal of the Season in 2008?

13. Chelsea sold Carlton Cole to which club in 2006?

14. How many goals did Lassana Diarra score in his Blues career?

15. Which country did Khalid Boulahrouz play for?

16. Against which team did Lewis Baker score Chelsea's Goal of the Season in 2013/14?

17. Who was the only team that Chris Sutton scored against for the Blues in the Premier League?

18. In what year did Jes Hogh make his Chelsea debut?

19. Which former Blue was the manager of Maccabi Tel Aviv against the Blues in the 2015/16 season?

20. Who was named the Chelsea Young Player of the Year in 2011/12?

Answers from quiz Milestones

1 Liverpool 2 Bradford City 3 Tommy Miller 4 2004 5 Bristol City 6 Preston 7 Walter Bettridge 8 Bobby Tambling 9 Liverpool 10 Bradford City 11 Peter Bonetti 12 Jason Cundy 13 1932 14 John Terry 15 Jack Cock 16 Everton 17 Kerry Dixon 18 West Brom 19 1905 20 2013

Chelsea By Definition

The questions below give a definition related to a surname in Chelsea history. Can you work out which player each question relates to?

1. Having or showing experience, knowledge, and good judgement.

2. A body of people (typically twelve in number) sworn to give a verdict in a legal case on the basis of evidence submitted to them in court.

3. The room or space just inside the front entrance of a house or flat.

4. An order to a bank to pay a stated sum from the drawer's account, written on a specially printed form.

5. A flour pudding boiled or steamed in a cloth bag.

6. A structure carrying a road, path, railway, etc. across a river, road, or other obstacle.

7. An eighth of a mile, 220 yards.

8. A counter in a pub, restaurant, or cafe across which drinks or refreshments are served.

9. The SI unit of power, equivalent to one joule per second, corresponding to the rate of consumption of energy in an electric circuit where the potential difference is one volt and the current one ampere.

10. A man who served his sovereign or lord as a mounted soldier in armour.

11. Move steadily and continuously in a current or stream.

12. A male peafowl, which has very long tail feathers that have eye-like markings and can be erected and fanned out in display.

13. Exchange or express diverging or opposite views, typically in a heated or angry way.

14. A wheel or other part in a mechanism that receives power directly and transmits motion to other parts.

15. A wreath of flowers and leaves, worn on the head or hung as a decoration.

16. Walk with long, decisive steps in a specified direction.

17. Happening quickly or promptly.

18. A very small patch of colour or light.

19. Agree to give or allow (something requested) to.

20. A large earthenware beer mug.

Answers from quiz General Knowledge 9

1 Yellow 2 Ross Turnbull 3 Seven 4 John Mikel Obi 5 Croatia 6 Striker 7 Blackburn Rovers 8 1950s 9 Jimmy Greaves 10 Wales 11 2014/15 12 Juliano Belletti 13 West Ham 14 Zero 15 Holland 16 Arsenal U21s 17 Manchester United 18 1999 19 Slavisa Jokanovic 20 Lucas Piazon

Kerry Dixon

Kerry Dixon was a star striker for Chelsea but how much do you know about one of the club's greatest ever goalscorers?

1. In which year did Kerry Dixon sign for Chelsea?

2. Which team did he score two goals against on his debut?

3. How many games did Dixon play for the Blues?

4. Which team were Chelsea's opponents in Kerry's final game for the Blues?

5. In which year did he play for England in the World Cup?

6. What was the title of his autobiography?

7. In 1983 Dixon missed two penalties for Chelsea in a game against which club?

8. How many hattricks did he score for the Blues?

9. Which Arsenal goalkeeper did Dixon score against in the opening fixture of the 1984/85 season?

10. Which team did Kerry score four goals against in an FA Cup 3rd round in 1985?

11. What country did he play against in his first international match?

12. How many goals did he score in the 1984/85 season?

13. What was his nickname at Chelsea?

14. Which team did he score more goals against than any other?

15. How many times did he captain the Blues?

16. Which team did he score his 100th Chelsea goal against?

17. Which team did Chelsea secure promotion against in 1985 with Dixon scoring a hattrick in a 5-0 win?

18. What was the name of the pub that he owned with Ian Hutchinson?

19. How much did Chelsea initially pay to sign Kerry Dixon?

20. Which striker did he play with at both Chelsea and Southampton?

Answers from quiz Chelsea By Definition

1 Dennis Wise 2 Gordon Durie 3 Gareth Hall 4 Petr Cech 5 Damien Duff 6 Wayne Bridge 7 Paul Furlong 8 Demba Ba 9 Steven Watt 10 Leon Knight 11 Tore Andre Flo 12 Gavin Peacock 13 Jimmy Argue 14 Phil Driver 15 Chris Garland 16 David Stride 17 John Swift 18 Robert Fleck 19 Anthony Grant 20 Mark Stein

Pre-WW2 Chelsea

This set of questions is all about Chelsea before WW2. How well do you know you club?

1. Who did the Blues play in their first competitive game at Stamford Bridge?

2. In what position did Chelsea finish in their first season?

3. Who did Chelsea play in their last competitive game in the 1938/39 season?

4. Which architect built Stamford Bridge?

5. From which club did Chelsea sign Hughie Gallacher?

6. Who was the Blues longest serving manager?

7. Who became the first person to score a hattrick for Chelsea?

8. Which Chelsea player became the club's first full international in 1906?

9. A league record crowd watched Chelsea vs Newcastle at Stamford Bridge

in 1909. What was the attendance?

10. In which year were the Blues first relegated?

11. Who was the first player to score 100 goals for Chelsea?

12. Which monarch watched Chelsea vs Leicester in 1920?

13. Which continent did the Blues travel to for a series of friendlies in 1929?

14. In which year did greyhound racing first appear at Stamford Bridge?

15. Chelsea's highest ever attendance in a league game was 82,905 back in 1935. Who were the opponents?

16. What nickname were Chelsea given after wearing shirt numbers?

17. How many people that played for Chelsea were killed during WW1?

18. What was the shade of blue that was used for Chelsea's first shirts?

19. Which team did the Blues beat 9-2 in the opening game of the 1906/07 season?

20. Which country did Willie Foulke represent?

Answers from quiz Kerry Dixon

1 1983 2 Derby County 3 420 4 Everton 5 1986 6 Kerry: The Autobiography 7 Portsmouth 8 Eight 9 Pat Jennings 10 Wigan 11 Mexico 12 36 13 The Wig 14 Oxford Utd 15 Zero 16 Aston Villa 17 Leeds Utd 18 The Union Inn 19 £150,000 20 David Speedie

Transfers

Transfers have always been a huge talking point for football fans. Take a look at these transfer related questions and try to answer them.

1. Who became the world's most expensive goalkeeper when he signed for Chelsea in 2018?

2. Which Italian signed for the Blues for a club record fee in 1996?

3. Which team bought Romelu Lukaku from Chelsea?

4. In 2013, which 40 year old goalkeeper signed for the Blues?

5. Who did Chelsea sign in 2011 and 2016?

6. Tore Andre Flo left the Blues to sign for which club?

7. Which manager sold Peter Osgood to Southampton?

8. Shaun Wright-Phillips left Chelsea to join which club?

9. In which year did Pat Nevin join Everton?

10. How much did Chelsea pay for Jimmy Floyd Hasselbaink in 2000?

11. Which player was involved in a transfer saga involving Lyn Oslo and Manchester Utd?

12. In which year did FIFA ban the Blues from making any signings for two transfer windows?

13. Who was Chelsea's first £100 signing?

14. Who became the Blues first £10,000 signing back in 1930?

15. Joe Cole left Chelsea to join which club?

16. In what year did Dan Petrescu sign for the Blues?

17. Andy Townsend left Chelsea to join which club?

18. Which manager signed Marcos Alonso?

19. Who left Chelsea in 1947 to join Third Division South club Notts County in a British record £20,000?

20. Who played in the 2014 Champions League final whilst on loan from the Blues?

Answers from quiz Pre-WW2 Chelsea

1 Hull City 2 Third 3 Bolton Wanderers 4 Archibald Leitch 5 Newcastle Utd 6 David Calderhead 7 Jimmy Windridge 8 Jack Kirwan 9 70000 10 1910 11 George Hilsdon 12 King George V 13 South America 14 1933 15 Arsenal 16 Los Numerados 17 Seven 18 Eton Blue 19 Glossop 20 England

Injuries

Injuries in football are common with some being career ending or life changing. How many of these injury related questions can you answer?

1. Against which team did Petr Cech sustain a head injury which led to him wearing a protective helmet for the rest of his career?

2. Which Reading player caused the injury?

3. Who broke his leg in a game vs St Gallen in 2000?

4. In which year did Paul Elliott have his career ending injury vs Liverpool?

5. Which Liverpool player injured his groin on the goal post for Pierluigi Casiraghi's only Chelsea goal?

6. Who retired after receiving a serious knee ligament injury in October 1987?

7. Ruben Loftus-Cheek suffered an injury in a friendly that kept him out of the 2019 Europa League final. Who were the opponents?

8. In 1996, which midfielder broke his leg in a collision with Kevin Hitchcock?

9. Which Hull City player was forced to retire after sustaining an injury during a head clash with Gary Cahill in 2017?

10. Who retired at Chelsea in 2004 after suffering several knee injuries?

11. In 1995, who sustained a head injury and later wore a head bandage whilst scoring two goals?

12. Who spent two months in a coma in 1997 after being hit by a car?

13. In 2007, who fractured a cheek bone vs Fulham and had to wear a face mask during his recovery?

14. Who retired through injury in 2001, aged just 32, and was called a 'Water Carrier' by Eric Cantona?

15. Which player was unable to chase back a Craig Burley back pass in the 1996 FA Cup semi-final as he had a hamstring injury?

16. Which player scored a penalty against Tottenham in 1996 before coming off with a broken leg?

17. In the 1993/94 season, who injured himself by dropping a 2kg jar of salad cream on his foot?

18. Which former Chelsea midfielder tore a knee ligament and missed five months of football after slipping in a puddle of his puppy's urine?

19. Who did Chelsea sign in 2004 but had a delayed debut after sustaining a broken metatarsal in a pre-season friendly vs Roma?

20. What career ending injury did Arthur Smith receive during World War II?

Answers from quiz Transfers

1 Kepa Arrizabalaga 2 Roberto Di Matteo 3 Everton 4 Mark Schwarzer 5 David Luiz 6 Rangers 7 Dave Sexton 8 Manchester City 9 1988 10 £15m 11 John Mikel Obi 12 2019 13 Bob McRoberts 14 Hughie Gallacher 15 Liverpool 16 1995 17 Aston Villa 18 Antonio Conte 19 Tommy Lawton 20 Thibaut Courtois

Stadiums

Chelsea have played in some of the world's best (and worst) stadiums. Try to answer these stadium related questions.

1. What was the name of the stadium where Chelsea played their first ever

competitive game?

2. In which stadium did Chelsea win the FA Cup in 1970?

3. In which city did the Blues play in the Luzhniki Stadium?

4. In what stadium did Chelsea play Liverpool in the 2019 UEFA Super Cup?

5. What is the name of the stadium where Frank Lampard scored his 203rd goal for the Blues?

6. In which stadium did Gianfranco Zola make his Chelsea debut?

7. Where did the Blues seal their first ever Premier League title?

8. In which stadium did Chelsea play away to Fulham in the 2003/04 season?

9. Which team did the Blues play at Leeds Road between 1911 and 1983?

10. In which stadium did Chelsea beat Wimbledon 3-0 in the 1997 FA Cup semi-final?

11. Who did the Blues play in the Karaiskaki Stadium in 1971?

12. In which stadium did Chelsea compete in their first FA Cup final in 1915?

13. In which country did the Blues beat Stuttgart in the Rasunda Stadium?

14. In which stadium did Chelsea win the 2013 Europa League final?

15. Selhurst Park held league matches against Chelsea for how many different teams between 1989 and 1990?

16. In which stadium did Eden Hazard make his Blues debut?

17. In which stadium did Pierluigi Casiraghi score his only Chelsea goal?

18. In which stadium did Radamel Falcao score his only Chelsea goal?

19. Gordon Durie scored five goals in one Chelsea game in which stadium?

20. John Terry received eight red cards in his Blues career. In which stadium was he sent off twice?

Answers from quiz Injuries

1 Reading 2 Stephen Hunt 3 Roberto Di Matteo 4 1992 5 Phil Babb 6 Eddie Niedzwiecki 7 New England Revolution 8 Eddie Newton 9 Ryan Mason 10 Emmanuel Petit 11 John Spencer 12 Alan Hudson 13 John Terry 14 Didier

Deschamps 15 Terry Phelan 16 David Lee 17 Dave Beasant 18 Darren Barnard 19 Arjen Robben 20 Fell off a kerb and foot was run over by a bus

True or False 8

Read the following questions. Just simply answer True or False for each question.

1. In 2016, Ruben Loftus-Cheek's house was struck by lightning.
2. Steve Francis had a daughter called Frances.
3. Emmanuel Petit scored in a World Cup final.
4. Didier Deschamps won the World Cup as a player and a manager.
5. Gordon Davies used to breed bearded dragons after he retired from football.
6. Diego Maradona played for Chelsea in a charity match in 1989.
7. In 1993, Ray Wilkins was awarded an MBE for services to Association Football.
8. Nick Crittenden was a goalkeeper for Chelsea in the 1990s.
9. Clive Allen played for seven different London clubs during his football career.
10. Bob Turnbull scored over 50 goals for the Blues.
11. John Bumstead had six toes on one foot.
12. England goalkeeper David James once scored against the Blues in an FA Cup match.
13. Chelsea striker Jack Cock starred in several films during the 1920s and 1930s.
14. Roman Abramovich used to sell rubber ducks.
15. Dennis Wise was once sent off for jokingly showing a referee a red card.
16. Ken Armstrong played international football for England as well as New Zealand.

17. In 1937, Chelsea became the first English club ever to participate in an international tournament.

18. In 2007, Frode Grodas was a contestant in the Norwegian version of The X Factor.

19. Paul Furlong scored more goals for the Blues than Andriy Shevchenko.

20. Tony Cottee scored in five consecutive games against Chelsea for West Ham between 1985 and 1986.

Answers from quiz Stadiums

1 Edgeley Park 2 Old Trafford 3 Moscow 4 Vodafone Park 5 Villa Park 6 Ewood Park 7 Reebok Stadium 8 Loftus Road 9 Huddersfield Town 10 Highbury 11 Real Madrid 12 Old Trafford 13 Sweden 14 Amsterdam ArenA 15 Three 16 Villa Park 17 Anfield 18 Stamford Bridge 19 Bescot Stadium 20 White Hart Lane

Missing Letters 2

Fill in the missing letters to reveal the name of someone from Chelsea's history.

1. _A_L _A_O_I_L_ (4,9)

2. _E_R_E _R_H_M (6,6)

3. _O_G _O_G_I_ (4,7)

4. _A_I_L _T_R_I_G_ (6,9)

5. _O_Y _O_E_ (4,5)

6. _I_N_U_A _I_L_I (8,6)

7. _E_A _R_I_A_A_A_A (4,12)

8. _A_L _U_L_N_ (4,7)

9. _M_A_U_L _E_I_ (8,5)

10. _E_N_N _R_S_O (6,6)

11. _O_S _A_K_E_ (4,7)

12. _L_A_O _O_A_A (6,6)

13. _L_N _O_N_O_ (4,7)

14. _U_D _U_L_T (4,6)

15. _A_K _T_I_ (4,5)

16. _O_E_T _U_H (6,4)

17. _Y_N _E_T_A_D (4,8)

18. _A_L _L_I_T_ (4,7)

19. _I_N_E _O_E_ (6,5)

20. _A_L _E_R_L_S (4,8)

1 True 2 False 3 True 4 True 5 False 6 False 7 True 8 False 9 True 10 True 11

False 12 False 13 True 14 True 15 False 16 True 17 True 18 False 19 False 20

True

Nobody Remembers Second

History only remembers the winners so can you name these questions about being in second place?

1. Who did Chelsea play in their second ever competitive game?

2. Who scored the Blues' second ever goal?

3. Who did Chelsea play in their second FA Cup final?

4. In what position did the Blues finish in their second competitive season?

5. Who has scored the second most goals for the club?

6. Who has made the second most appearances for Chelsea?

7. Who was the club's second ever manager?

8. Who was the second player to score a Premier League hattrick for Chelsea?

9. Who was the second person to be sent off for the Blues?

10. How many times have Chelsea finished second in the top flight?

11. Who scored the second goal for the Blues in the 2019 Europa League final?

12. Jose Mourinho was the 'Special One' but who did he appoint as Assistant Manager when he first joined the club?

13. Who did Frank Lampard score his second goal against?

14. Who was the second person to win the Chelsea Player of the Year award?

15. What colour was Chelsea's away shirt in the 1905/06 season?

16. How many seasons in total have the Blues' played in the second tier of English football?

17. Who was Chelsea's second ever shirt sponsor?

18. Who is the second youngest person to play for Chelsea?

19. Who is the second oldest person to play for Chelsea?

20. Who was the second black player to make an appearance for the club?

Answers from quiz Missing Letters 2

1 Paul Canoville 2 George Graham 3 Doug Rougvie 4 Daniel Sturridge 5 Joey Jones 6 Gianluca Vialli 7 Kepa Arrizabalaga 8 Paul Furlong 9 Emmanuel Petit 10 Hernan Crespo 11 Ross Barkley 12 Alvaro Morata 13 Glen Johnson 14 Ruud Gullit 15 Mark Stein 16 Robert Huth 17 Ryan Bertrand 18 Paul Elliott 19 Vinnie Jones 20 Raul Meireles

General Knowledge 10

This round tests your Chelsea general knowledge. These are questions that most Blues fans should know but how many will you get correct?

1. In what year did Chelsea get their first 3 points for a league win?

2. Who were the Blues first ever opponents in the FA Cup?

3. Who was the Chelsea captain in the 1986 Full Members Cup final?

4. How many Englishmen played in the 2012 Champions League final?

5. Who knocked Chelsea out of the 2007/08 FA Cup?

6. In which season did Graeme Le Saux make his Blues debut?

7. Chelsea played their first League Cup match in 1960. Who were the opponents?

8. What country did Paulo Ferreira play for?

9. In 1999 which former Blue scored an own goal with Leicester against Chelsea?

10. Who many goals did Jimmy Greaves score against Wolves in August 1958?

11. Who were the first English side that Chelsea played in European competition?

12. In which country did the Blues play Videoton in the 2018/19 Europa League?

13. In which decade did Chelsea first play Bournemouth?

14. Who scored twice as the Blues beat Newcastle at Wembley in the 1999/00 FA Cup semi-final?

15. In 1961 Dixie Dean scored five goals against Chelsea in a single match. Who was he playing for?

16. What squad number did Yossi Benayoun wear in the 2010/11 season?

17. Which team did Chelsea used to play at the Goldstone Ground?

18. In 2011 Michael Mancienne left the Blues to play football in which country?

19. In what year did Jody Morris make his Chelsea debut?

20. In 2019 who became England's youngest ever player to make his debut in a competitive match?

Answers from quiz Nobody Remembers Second

1 Blackpool 2 David Copeland 3 Tottenham 4 2nd 5 Bobby Tambling 6 Peter Bonetti 7 William Lewis 8 Mark Hughes 9 Jack Harrow 10 Four 11 Pedro 12 Steve Clarke 13 Bolton Wanderers 14 Charlie Cooke 15 White 16 19 17 Grange Farm 18 Kingsley Whiffen 19 Dick Spence 20 Keith Jones

Almost Impossible 3

This set of questions are as the title suggests. How many of these almost impossible questions can you get correct?

1. Who did the Blues play in Kevin Hitchcock's testimonial?

2. In 1986, Chelsea played a testimonial at Craven Cottage against Fulham for which goalkeeper?

3. Which South African team did Tony Potrac, Joe Fascione and George Luke all leave the Blues to join?

4. How many games did Chelsea play in the 1945/46 season?

5. Who did the Blues beat in the 1956 FA Cup 4th round which included four replays?

6. Which manager sent several players home after breaking a curfew in Blackpool back in 1965?

7. Who said, "I may be one of the worst buys in the history of the Premiership, but I don't care."?

8. Which former Blue was given a 15 year horse racing ban back in 2013?

9. How many headed goals did John Terry score for Chelsea?

10. In which year did the Blues first name 11 internationals in their starting line-up?

11. In 1999, what item was thrown from the stands and hit referee Paul Durkin in a match with Oldham?

12. How many times was Ron Harris sent off for the Blues?

13. Which international country did Rati Aleksidze represent?

14. What is the name of Roman Abramovich's eldest son?

15. Who was Chelsea chairman from 1981 until 1982?

16. What is the name of the Mayfair Italian restaurant owned by stars Willian and David Luiz?

17. Colin Viljoen won international caps with which country?

18. In what year did Chelsea's mascot Stamford the Lion first appear?

19. In April 1991 which club tried to sign Kerry Dixon on loan?

20. Which former Blue has Brian Mears as a father-in-law?

Answers from quiz General Knowledge 10

1 1981 2 1st Grenadiers 3 Colin Pates 4 Four 5 Barnsley 6 1988/89 7 Millwall 8 Portugal 9 Frank Sinclair 10 Five 11 Manchester City 12 Hungary 13 1980s 14 Gus Poyet 15 Everton 16 Ten 17 Brighton & Hove Albion 18 Germany 19 1996 20 Callum Hudson-Odoi

Answers from quiz Almost Impossible 3

1 Nottingham Forest 2 Gerry Peyton 3 Durban City 4 Six 5 Burnley 6 Tommy Docherty 7 Winston Bogarde 8 Neil Clement 9 45 10 1998 11 Hotdog 12 Zero 13 Georgia 14 Arkadiy 15 Charles Cadogan 16 Inside Babbo 17 England 18 1980 19 Real Madrid 20 Steve Wicks

GATE 17
THE COMPLETE COLLECTION
(CHRISTMAS 2020)

CHELSEA

Over Land and Sea – Mark Worrall
Chelsea here, Chelsea There – Kelvin Barker, David Johnstone, Mark Worrall
Chelsea Football Fanzine – the best of cfcuk
One Man Went to Mow – Mark Worrall
Chelsea Chronicles (Five Volume Series) – Mark Worrall
Making History Not Reliving It –
Kelvin Barker, David Johnstone, Mark Worrall
Celery! Representing Chelsea in the 1980s – Kelvin Barker
Stuck On You: a year in the life of a Chelsea supporter – Walter Otton
Palpable Discord: a year of drama and dissent at Chelsea – Clayton Beerman
Rhyme and Treason – Carol Ann Wood
Eddie Mac Eddie Mac – Eddie McCreadie's Blue & White Army
The Italian Job: A Chelsea thriller starring Antonio Conte – Mark Worrall
Carefree! Chelsea Chants & Terrace Culture – Mark Worrall, Walter Otton
Diamonds, Dynamos and Devils – Tim Rolls
Arrivederci Antonio: The Italian Job (part two) – Mark Worrall
Where Were You When We Were Shocking? – Neil L. Smith
Chelsea: 100 Memorable Games – Chelsea Chadder
Bewitched, Bothered & Bewildered – Carol Ann Wood
Stamford Bridge Is Falling Down – Tim Rolls
Cult Fiction – Dean Mears
Chelsea: If Twitter Was Around When… – Chelsea Chadder
Blue Army – Vince Cooper
Liquidator 1969-70 A Chelsea Memoir – Mark Worrall
When Skies Are Grey: Super Frank, Chelsea And The Coronavirus Crisis – Mark Worrall
Tales Of The (Chelsea) Unexpected – David Johnstone & Neil L Smith
The Ultimate Unofficial Chelsea Quiz Book – Chelsea Chadder
Blue Days – Chris Wright
Let The Celery Decide – Walter Otton

FICTION

Blue Murder: Chelsea Till I Die – Mark Worrall
The Wrong Outfit – Al Gregg
The Red Hand Gang – Walter Otton
Coming Clean – Christopher Morgan
This Damnation – Mark Worrall
Poppy – Walter Otton

NON FICTION

Roe2Ro – Walter Otton
Shorts – Walter Otton
England International Football Team Quiz & Trivia Book – George Cross

www.gate17.co.uk

Printed in Great Britain
by Amazon

51020894R00087